SPLIT-DIAMOND
DAZZLERS

SPLIT-DIAMOND
DAZZLERS

QUILTS TO PAPER PIECE

PAULINE JOHNSTON

Martingale™
& COMPANY

Credits

President ❖ Nancy J. Martin

CEO ❖ Daniel J. Martin

Publisher ❖ Jane Hamada

Editorial Director ❖ Mary V. Green

Managing Editor ❖ Tina Cook

Technical Editor ❖ Laurie Baker

Copy Editor ❖ Liz McGehee

Design Director ❖ Stan Green

Illustrator ❖ Laurel Strand

Cover and Text Designer ❖ Regina Girard

Photographer ❖ Brent Kane

That Patchwork Place® is an imprint
of Martingale & Company™.

Split-Diamond Dazzlers: Quilts to Paper Piece
© 2003 by Pauline Johnston

Martingale & Company
20205 144th Avenue NE
Woodinville, WA 98072-8478 USA
www.martingale-pub.com

Printed in China
08 07 06 05 04 03   8 7 6 5 4 3 2 1

Mission Statement

We are dedicated to providing quality products and service by working together to inspire creativity and to enrich the lives we touch.

Library of Congress Cataloging In-Publication Data
Johnston, Pauline
    Split-diamond dazzlers : quilts to paper piece / Pauline Johnston.
      p. cm.
    ISBN 1-56477-469-4
   1. Patchwork—Patterns. 2. Quilting. 3. Patchwork quilts.
I. Title.
    TT835 .J645 2003
    746.46—dc21
                          2002151276

DEDICATION

In memory of Mij and Polo, my beloved cats, both sadly missed.

ACKNOWLEDGMENTS

Many thanks to Michael Holmes for helping me draft the foundation pattern and for his time and patience. Thank you to my friends Judith Holden, Sheila Cope, and Rosemary Lowe, and to my cousin Pat Hodgkinson for their encouragement and support. A special thank-you to my late mother, Marion, for teaching me to sew and for instilling in me her motto: You can do anything if you try.

CONTENTS

INTRODUCTION

Twinkle, twinkle, little star,
How I wonder what you are.
Up above the world so high,
Like a diamond in the sky.
Twinkle, twinkle, little star,
How I wonder what you are!

I like to apply the lines in this charming little childhood rhyme to Split Diamonds—the units that I use for the quilts in this book.

Twinkle, twinkle, little star . . . A little star made from eight Split Diamonds will certainly twinkle (or twirl) because the diamonds that make up the star are made from three different fabrics. At least eight original designs can be made from various combinations and arrangements of these eight diamonds; many more original designs become available when more diamonds are added to the points of the star. And they are all guaranteed to twinkle. Most of the designs are based on much-loved, traditional, eight-pointed star patterns, such as Virginia Star, Sunburst, and Rolling Star, but using Split Diamonds, instead of diamonds cut from one fabric, brings a whole new and creative dimension to an already popular group of designs.

How I wonder what you are . . . Split Diamonds are 45° diamonds that are made from simple foundation-pieced Diamond Log Cabin units. These units, along with background pieces, are all you need to make the blocks for the designs in this book. After piecing the Diamond Log Cabin units, you will cut them into quarters, with each unit yielding four Split Diamonds. Two of the diamonds will have Log Cabin strips along the two adjacent sides that meet at the 45° angle. These will be referred to as Twinkling diamonds. The other two diamonds will have Log Cabin strips along the two adjacent sides meeting at the 135° angle. We will call these Twirling diamonds. A design can be made from all Twinkling diamonds, all Twirling diamonds, or a combination of both.

Up above the world so high . . . Accomplishing a beautiful and intricate quilt has always made me feel on top of the world, but many quilters shy away from designs made from 45° diamonds because they think they are too difficult to draft or sew. With Split Diamonds, drafting is eliminated because all the patterns in this book are made from one foundation-pieced unit and all the diamonds are the same size. Sewing lines are marked on all the diamonds, and alignment dots are marked on both the diamonds and the background pieces, which takes most of the guesswork out of that dreaded ¼" seam allowance. With this accurate method, perfect piecing is easily accomplished.

Like a diamond in the sky . . . The sky's the limit when designing with Split Diamonds because there are so many different ways in which Twinkling and Twirling diamonds can be arranged. When these arrangements are combined with color, contrast, and texture, the design possibilities are endless.

NOTE
The diamonds you see at the beginning of each project indicate the difficulty level of the project, with one diamond being the easiest and three diamonds being the most difficult.

◆ Easiest
◆ ◆ Moderate
◆ ◆ ◆ Advanced

PREPARING TO PIECE THE DIAMOND LOG CABIN UNITS

You'll need to know some basic information before you can start foundation-piecing the units needed for the projects. In this section, you'll learn about selecting foundation material and fabric, how to make the foundation patterns, what the markings mean on the pattern, and how to cut the fabric pieces for the foundation units.

Choosing a Foundation Material

You have several options when it comes to the material you can use to trace the Diamond Log Cabin foundation pattern, just a few of which are mentioned here. If you are familiar with foundation-piecing techniques and prefer another material, by all means use it.

Tracing Paper

Thin tracing paper makes an ideal foundation for machine piecing. I prefer to use dressmaker's tissue paper, the type used for making commercial clothing patterns. Depending on where you live, you can find it either in large sheets, approximately 18" x 27", or on 60' rolls. It is strong enough to withstand a fair amount of handling, but tears away easily so the pieced top can be hand quilted if desired.

Foundation Piecing Paper

Several companies manufacture blank papers specifically for foundation piecing. These papers absorb ink quickly, tear away easily from fabric, and are semi-transparent, allowing you to see the fabrics through the paper. The papers are suitable for use with most photocopiers and ink-jet and laser printers, but if you intend to photocopy the foundation pattern, be sure the copier produces accurate copies. Distortion is a problem with many copiers, and if the foundation pattern is distorted in any way, the background pieces will not be compatible.

Interfacing

Lightweight, nonwoven, nonfusible interfacing is the best type to use for foundation piecing. The foundation pattern can be traced directly onto it, and the interfacing will keep its shape during both sewing and pressing. You do not need to remove the interfacing after sewing, but leaving it attached will make hand quilting more difficult. If you use interfacing for your foundations, machine quilting might be a better option.

Selecting Fabrics

Yardage requirements for the projects in this book are based on 42" of usable fabric after preshrinking. Three different fabrics are always used to make the blocks: one fabric is used for the block center diamond, one for the first round of strips (logs) around the diamond, and another for the second round. With foundation piecing, you can use a variety of unusual fabrics to add extra interest to a design. The subtle sheen and texture of silk, the metallic glint of gold or silver lamé, and the shine of satin can all add vibrancy to a design (see "Stained Glass" on page 55 and "Shimmering Star" on page 70). However, you do need to consider the fabric color and print.

Color

There are no secrets about color. It is all a matter of personal taste. We all see color differently, and we all have a favorite color that we find ourselves using time and time again in our quiltmaking. While a color wheel has its purpose, I think it sometimes can be confusing for quilters to use because it only provides samples of flat colors. However, with a good selection of fabric samples, you also can consider design, scale, and texture. Choose the colors that you like, put them together, and you will probably be pleasantly surprised at the result.

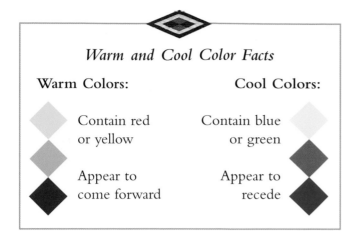

If you find it difficult to put several fabrics together, first choose a multicolored print that appeals to you, then choose additional fabrics that match the colors in the print fabric, considering the color value and contrast. Value is the degree of lightness and darkness of colors. Contrast is created when fabrics of different values are put together. The strongest contrasts are between light and dark and can create a sense of space and depth in a design, making some logs and diamonds advance while others recede. Follow these guidelines when considering color value for your blocks:

◆ Dark logs and diamonds appear to stand out more than lighter logs and diamonds, especially when placed next to light logs.

◆ Light logs seem to spread into darker logs and appear wider than dark logs of the same width. Dark logs placed next to light logs appear to contract.

◆ Light diamonds appear larger than dark diamonds of equal size, especially when placed next to dark logs.

◆ Dark colors appear heavier than light colors.

◆ Value is a relative term. The same fabric might be a dark value in one situation but a medium value in another.

◆ Strong color contrasts appear to stand out while weaker ones recede.

Split Diamonds can be made from colors that blend into one another (see "Star Flower" on page 73), colors that contrast (see "Stained Glass" on page 55), or colors that blend in some parts of the diamond and contrast in others (see "Wreathed Star" on page 69). To create a visual effect of spaces within the diamonds, use the background fabric in some of the logs and diamonds (see "Stained Glass" on page 55).

Print

The printed pattern on a fabric will change the intensity of colors and influence which logs and diamonds contrast with each other and which blend together. Fabric patterns are divided into three categories: type, scale, and density.

Pattern type may be geometric, floral, dots, paisley—to name just a few—and is determined by the way the pattern is printed on the background. Allover prints have the design placed at random and are ideal for Split Diamonds because the design isn't affected by the grain line. A geometric layout places the design on the background in either horizontal, vertical, or diagonal rows. The design doesn't always correspond to the fabric grain and is often one-way; stripes and checks are included in this category. Used with care, geometric prints can often add interest to a quilt, but with Split Diamonds, it is wise to avoid directional prints, such as stripes and checks or any obvious one-way pattern. When the foundation blocks are cut apart, it is impossible to predict which way a directional design will lie in each log or diamond.

Scale is how large or small the type of pattern is. A flower might be a full-blown rose or a tiny bud. Small patterns give a calmer feeling and are often just two colors or a tone-on-tone print. These are especially useful with Split Diamonds because their scale and density adds variety and helps to establish a design. Medium-scale prints and small multicolored prints will provide visual texture. Large patterns have more movement and are frequently found in multiple colors, but because the Log Cabin strips in the foundation block are very narrow, large-scale prints aren't able to "show" themselves. However, this doesn't mean you can't use some larger-scale prints; they can sometimes add contrast and character to a design and they can be very effective in a border.

Density is often called the "busyness" of a print fabric. How busy a design is depends on how much background is showing between the elements of a design. If a design is widely spaced, it is less busy than a design printed close together. A solid color with little or no print at all has more density than a floral print. Avoid using too many busy prints in Split Diamonds or they will all blend together. One or two busy prints is usually enough.

When selecting a fabric for the background pieces, avoid directional designs or fabrics that demand attention. Fabrics that complement your blocks, but do not detract from them, are best.

Understanding the Pattern Markings

The illustration shown here is a smaller version of the full-size pattern on page 10. You will notice that there are black solid lines, red solid lines, black broken lines, and dots, as well as a shaded area. It is important to know what each of these markings means before you begin piecing.

◆ Black solid lines within the foundation pattern are sewing lines used to piece the foundation unit. The outside solid lines indicate where to trim the unit after piecing.

◆ Red solid lines are cutting lines used to divide the foundation block into four Split Diamonds.

◆ Black broken lines are seam lines used to sew the diamonds together or to set in background pieces.

◆ Dots marked on the foundation pattern are used for alignment, providing accuracy when sewing diamonds together and setting in background pieces.

◆ The shaded area in the center of the pattern defines the area where the fabric for the center diamond will be placed.

◆ The numbers indicate the sewing sequence for the log strips.

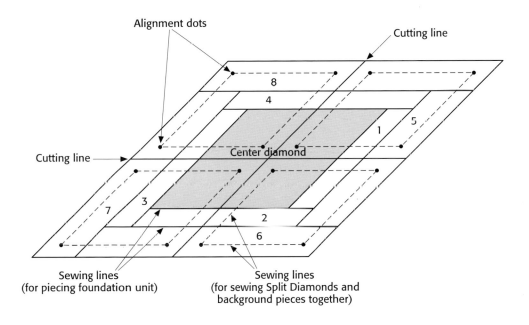

Preparing to Piece the Diamond Log Cabin Units 9

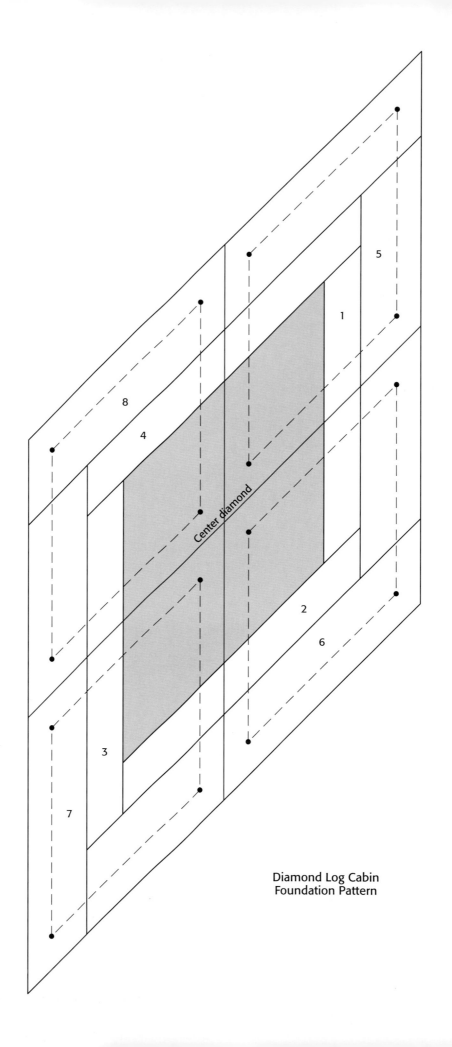

Center diamond

5

1

8

4

2

6

3

7

Diamond Log Cabin
Foundation Pattern

Transferring the Pattern to the Foundation Material

Trace the pattern on page 10 onto the desired foundation material exactly as given, using a 6"-long ruler to make straight lines. The ¼" seam allowance has already been included, so there is no need to add it. Transfer all solid lines, broken lines, numbers, and alignment dots. It is not necessary to mark the red solid lines with a red pen or pencil, but you may find it helpful as long as you remember that they are cutting lines and not sewing lines. You also do not need to shade the area for the center diamond, but again, you may find it helpful to define it in some way.

Each project will indicate the number of foundations needed. If you are tracing each pattern by hand, use a mechanical pencil or a sharp lead pencil. If you plan to photocopy the patterns, trace the pattern onto a sheet of typing paper, using a fine-line ink pen, and use the traced pattern to make the photocopies. You can copy directly from the book, but books do not always lie flat, and you could end up with a distorted pattern. Always check the first copy to make sure the copier is not distorting the pattern before you make additional copies.

If you are using large sheets of tracing paper or interfacing, cut them into manageable pieces. I find that cutting 5" x 11" rectangles is more convenient than cutting diamonds, and rectangles are also much easier to handle. The excess foundation paper is trimmed when the block is complete.

Cutting the Foundation Unit Pieces

Unlike traditional foundation piecing, the fabric pieces needed to make the Diamond Log Cabin unit—the center diamond and eight log strips—are precut so that the fabric grain line can be maintained. Fabric grain line is often ignored during foundation piecing because the foundation stabilizes the fabrics. However, I find it very irritating to the eye if a foundation block is made up of fabric pieces that have been pieced so that the grain line is lying all higgledy-piggledy. With Split Diamonds, it is impossible to predict which way the grain will lie when the diamonds are arranged in a design, but it is possible to make the grain lines lie in the same direction in all of the diamonds, which will give some sort of order to your finished project.

The lengthwise grain line runs parallel to the selvage edges of the fabric, and the crosswise grain line runs from selvage to selvage. Log Cabin strips can be cut from either the lengthwise grain or the crosswise grain, but I prefer to cut them along the crosswise grain because it has a little more give, or stretch, than the lengthwise grain. It is also a more economical way of using my precious fabric.

True bias is cut at a 45° angle to the selvage, and it is the stretchiest part of the fabric. The 45° diamond has two sets of parallel lines for its sides; two sides are on the bias, while the other two sides are on the straight grain. Although the give on the bias edges is not very important with foundation piecing, if you can cut and place all the center diamonds so that they are going in the same direction on the foundation paper, when the blocks are split, all the Twinkling diamonds will have the straight grain on one side of the center diamonds, and all the Twirling diamonds will have the straight grain on the opposite side of the center diamond.

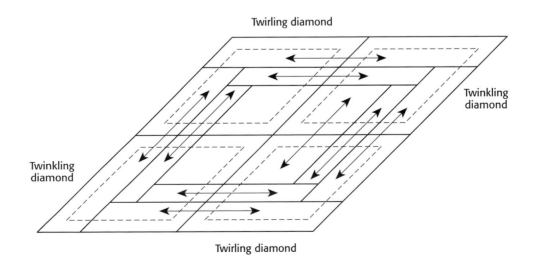

Twirling diamond

Twinkling diamond

Twinkling diamond

Twinkling diamond

Twirling diamond

Cutting the Center 45° Diamond

1. Lay the fabric you have selected for the center diamonds, wrong side up, on the cutting mat.
2. Using a rotary cutter and ruler, cut a strip of fabric 2½" wide across the straight grain of the fabric.
3. Align the 45° line of the ruler with the top edge of the strip, and cut along the right edge of the ruler.

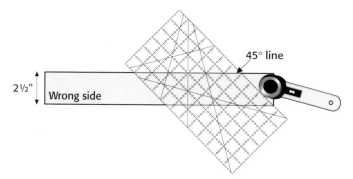

4. Turn the strip so that the diagonally cut end is on the left, keeping the wrong side up. Align the 2½" line of the ruler with the diagonal edge, and the 45° line with the top edge of the strip; cut along the right edge of the ruler to release the diamond.

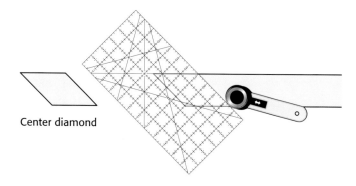

5. To cut additional diamonds from the strip, position the ruler as in step 4 as many times as needed to cut the desired amount of diamonds. The wrong side of the fabric strip must always be facing up, or the grain will be the reverse of the grain needed.

Cutting the Log Strips

Cutting the log strips precisely is not that important, provided the strips are large enough to cover the area marked on the foundation, but all of the strips should be cut across the fabric width (from selvage to selvage) to maintain the grain line. I cut all the strips for the first round of the block ⅞" wide, but if you prefer, you can cut them slightly wider. The finished width of the sewn strips is ⅜", so cutting the strips ⅞" wide allows ½" for seam allowances, which I find adequate. If you are inexperienced at foundation piecing, you may find that cutting a wider strip will avoid any need to restitch the seam because the strip finishes too narrow. Cut the strips for the second round of the block at least 1" wide. You will need the extra width to make sure the strip covers the ¼" seam allowance along the outside edges of the block.

Tip

You may use the sew-and-cut method, in which you use long strips to piece the block, cutting them off after you have sewn them to the foundation. If you prefer this method, I recommend that you do not cut the strips until after you have pressed them open and checked that they cover the correct area marked on the foundation. Otherwise, you may find that you have cut them too short.

Pressing

It is important to press every strip into place after you have sewn it to the foundation and before you add another strip. It is also important to press the completed block before trimming the outside edges and splitting it into four diamonds. You may not be able to trim the block accurately if it isn't pressed well. I prefer to use a steam iron, but steam can make paper foundations curl. To correct curling, turn the foundation over and press again from the paper side, this time without steam.

Now that you know what you'll need to piece the foundation units, gather your foundation material, ⅛ yard each of three fabrics, and your normal sewing supplies. The instructions here are for making two Diamond Log Cabin units. Later, we will cut the units apart and add background pieces to complete a sample block. Begin by tracing two foundation patterns (page 10) onto the selected foundation material. Then cut the center diamonds and log strips as follows:

From the center diamond fabric, cut:
1 strip, 2½" x width of fabric; from the strip, cut 2 center diamonds (see "Cutting the Center 45° Diamond" on page 12)

From the round 1 fabric for the Log Cabin strips, cut:
1 strip, ⅞" x width of fabric. From this strip, cut:
- ❖ 2 strips, 4" long, for log #1
- ❖ 4 strips, 4½" long, for logs #2 and #3
- ❖ 2 strips, 5" long, for log #4

From the round 2 fabric for the Log Cabin strip, cut:
2 strips, 1" x width of fabric. From these strips, cut:
- ❖ 2 strips, 5" long, for log #5
- ❖ 4 strips, 6" long, for logs #6 and #7
- ❖ 2 strips, 7" long, for log #8

1. Place the center diamond, right side up, over the center diamond area on the *unmarked* side of the foundation. While holding the fabric in place, turn the foundation to the marked side, and hold it up to the light to make sure the piece covers the center diamond area and extends ¼" beyond the marked area on all sides. Ignore the broken lines that intersect the center diamond for now. When satisfied with the placement, pin the diamond to the foundation using 2 straight pins.

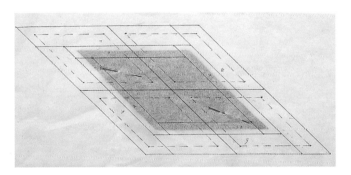

Center Diamond

Tip
If your foundation is transparent, you might find it easier to place the center diamond, wrong side up, on a flat surface and then position the foundation on top, with the marked side up. Make sure the center diamond extends ¼" beyond the marked area before pinning it in place.

2. With right sides together, place the log #1 strip on top of the center diamond. Align the raw edges of the center diamond and log strip, and make sure the log's excess length extends toward the narrow point of the diamond as shown. When the log is stitched in placed and pressed open, it should be long enough to cover the whole area marked "1" on the foundation, with at least ¼" extra for seam allowance. Pin the strip in place. If you are using interfacing for your foundation, set the stitch length at 12 to 15 stitches per inch; for a paper foundation, set the stitch length at 15 to 20 stitches per inch. With the marked side of the foundation up, sew directly on the solid seam line between the center diamond and log #1. Begin sewing two or three stitches before the line begins, and extend a few stitches at the end of the line. There is no need to backstitch because the stitches will be secured by the next sewing line. If necessary, trim the seam allowance to a scant ¼", but not less than ⅛".

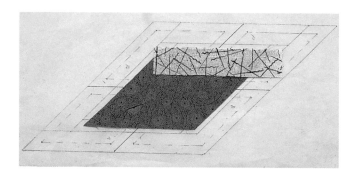

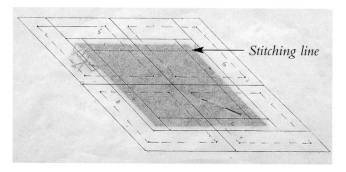

Stitching line

Log #1

3. Flip log #1 over so the right side faces up and covers the area marked "1" on the foundation. Hold the foundation up to the light again to make sure the log extends beyond the drawn lines. Pay particular attention to the pointed end

of the diamond; the extended log should be long enough to cover it with at least ¼" to spare. Press. Pin the strip in place if necessary.

4. Working counterclockwise, place the log #2 strip on top of the center diamond, right sides together, as shown. Align the raw edges of the center diamond and log strip, and make sure the log's excess length is placed toward the narrow point of the diamond. Pin the strip in place. Turn the foundation over and sew exactly on the solid seam line between the center diamond and log #2. Trim the seam allowance and any ears that protrude from the previous log.

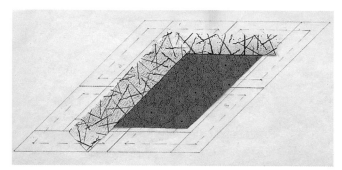

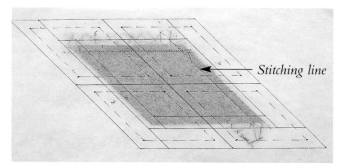

Stitching line

Log #2

5. Press the log over the area marked "2" and check that it extends beyond the lines, especially at the pointed end of the diamond, as in step 3.

Tip
Try to get into the habit of cutting off any loose threads as you trim the seam allowances. This will eliminate a tedious job after the blocks are finished.

6. Continue working counterclockwise around the center diamond to add the remaining round 1 logs and then the round 2 logs in the same manner. Always place the strip's excess length toward the narrow pointed end of the diamond.

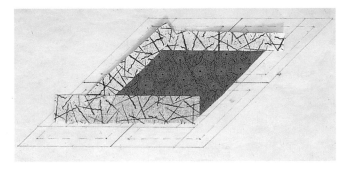

Log #3

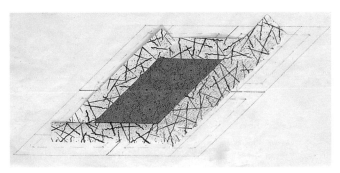

Log #4

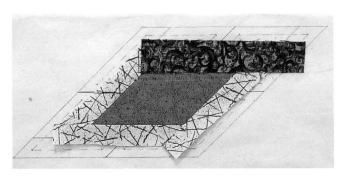

Log #5

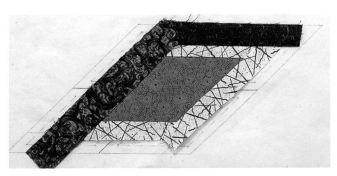

Log #6

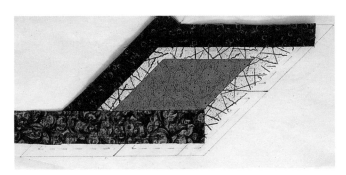

Log #7

Log #8

7. Press the completed unit. Turn the unit to the foundation's marked side. Trim the unit along the outer solid lines.

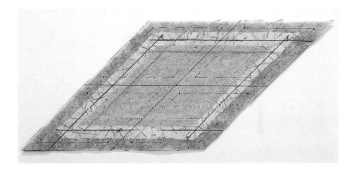

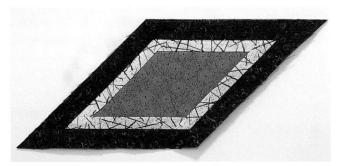

Completed Unit

8. Repeat steps 1–7 to make the second unit.
9. Follow the instructions in "Making a Sample Block" on page 21 to use the units in a block.

SPLITTING THE FOUNDATION UNITS

To split the pieced foundation units into four Split Diamonds, cut along the two red solid lines (refer to the original foundation pattern if necessary), using a rotary cutter or a sharp pair of scissors. I find scissors more accurate in this case.

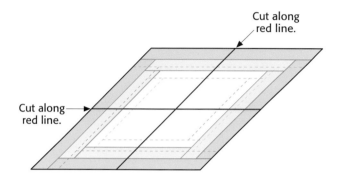

Cut along red line.

Cut along red line.

You will now notice that you have two different kinds of Split Diamonds. For ease of identification, Split Diamonds with a small diamond at the 45° angle have been named Twinkling diamonds; Split Diamonds with a small diamond at the 135° angle have been named Twirling diamonds. It is easy to remember which diamond is which because when you sew eight diamonds of the same type together to form a star, they will either twinkle or twirl.

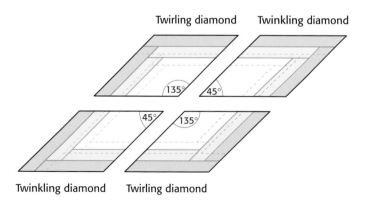

Twirling diamond   Twinkling diamond

135°   45°

45°   135°

Twinkling diamond   Twirling diamond

Twinkling Diamonds

Twirling Diamonds

One Diamond Log Cabin foundation unit will split into two Twinkling diamonds and two Twirling diamonds. The direction of the logs on both Twirling diamonds will be identical, but the direction of the logs on the Twinkling diamonds will be opposite each other. When the diamonds are sewn together, this is not very noticeable, but if you are a perfectionist, you may want to keep one-way diamonds together, in the same point of a star for instance. Then you can use the opposing diamonds in alternate star points.

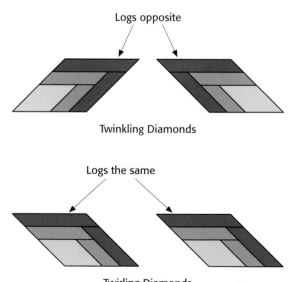

Logs opposite

Twinkling Diamonds

Logs the same

Twirling Diamonds

CUTTING AND MARKING THE BACKGROUND PIECES

While diamonds are the focus of the blocks in this book, you will need to cut background pieces to make the blocks square. You will also need background pieces for diamonds used in the borders. The instructions given here are for rotary cutting the pieces, but you can use the template patterns on pages 74–78 if you prefer. Regardless of the method you choose for cutting out the background pieces, after the pieces are cut, you will use the templates to mark the alignment dots on each background piece.

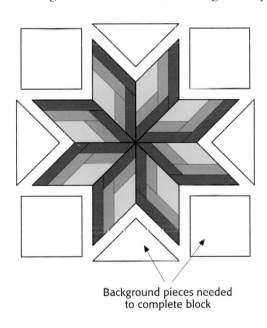

Background pieces needed
to complete block

Cutting

The pattern instructions for each project will indicate the number of each background piece needed to complete the block. You will not need every shape for every quilt.

Squares

Cut squares ½" larger than the size of the finished square. For example, if you need a 2" finished square, cut a 2½" square. To cut squares, cut a strip of fabric ½" wider than the finished size of the square. Turn the strip horizontally. Align the required measurement on the ruler, which should be the same as the strip width, with the left edge of the strip. Make sure a horizontal line on the ruler is aligned with the bottom edge of the strip to ensure a straight cut, and then cut along the right edge of the ruler.

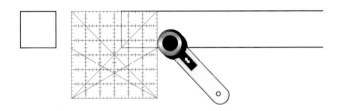

Right-Angle Triangles

It is important to distinguish between two kinds of right-angle triangles because they are both the same shape. The practical difference is the way the fabric grain lines are arranged: half-square triangles have the straight grain of the fabric along the two short sides of the triangle; quarter-square triangles have the straight grain along the longest side of the triangle. When you are positioning triangles within a block or block unit, the straight grain should always be placed along the outer edge of the block or block unit.

Quarter-square
triangles

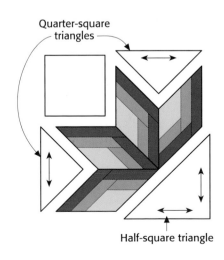

Half-square triangle

To cut two half-square triangles, first cut a square ⅞" larger than the desired finished size of the leg of the triangle, then cut the square in half once diagonally.

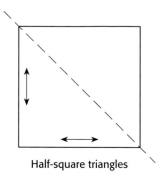

Half-square triangles

To cut four quarter-square triangles, first cut a square 1¼" larger than the finished size of the longest side of the triangle. Cut the square in half twice diagonally.

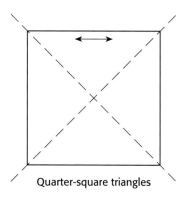

Quarter-square triangles

Diamonds

Whole diamonds, used as part of the background or used instead of Split Diamonds in a design, must finish to the same size as the Split Diamonds. The method is similar to cutting the center diamond for the Diamond Log Cabin foundation unit (see page 12), but instead of cutting 2½"-wide strips and diamonds, cut the strips and diamonds for background pieces 2" wide. With background diamonds, you may have to fold the strip in half widthwise to cut both diamonds and reversed diamonds.

Half Diamonds

Half diamonds are 45° diamonds that have been cut in half horizontally. To cut half diamonds, you must first cut a strip of fabric. From this strip, you will cut parallelograms, which are in turn cut once diagonally to yield two half diamonds.

1. Cut a 2⅞"-wide strip of fabric.
2. Refer to "Making the Templates and Marking the Background Pieces" on page 20 to trace template pattern F on page 78 onto frosted template plastic and cut it out. Using double-stick tape, attach it to the wrong side of a 6"-wide rotary ruler as shown, making sure the angled edge is flush with the edge of the ruler.

Template F

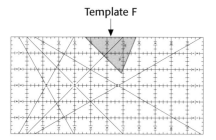

3. Place the ruler on the fabric strip so the bottom edge of the template is aligned with the bottom edge of the fabric strip. Cut along the right edge of the ruler to angle the strip end.

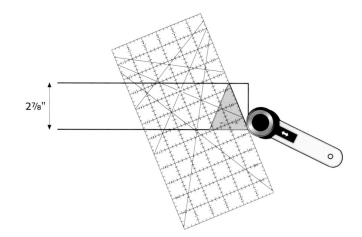

2⅞"

4. Turn the strip so the angled edge is to the left as shown. Remove the template from the ruler. Place the 2¼" line of the ruler on the cut edge and cut along the ruler's right edge to produce a parallelogram.

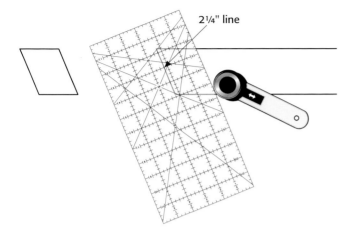

5. Cut the parallelogram in half as shown to produce two half diamonds.

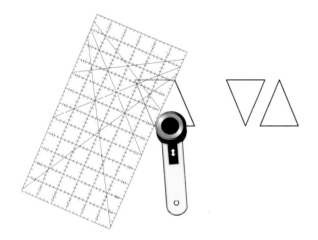

Corner Pieces

Corner pieces and reversed corner pieces are needed to complete a border made of vertically set Split Diamonds and half diamonds. Although you will not need these pieces for any of the projects given in this book, if you wish to add a border like that found on "Garden Maze" on page 71 of the photo gallery, the following corner piece is what you will use.

1. Cut a 2½"-wide strip of fabric along the fabric width. Fold the strip in half widthwise, wrong sides together. Cutting two corner pieces together will yield one corner piece and one reversed corner piece.
2. Align the 45° line of the ruler with the top edge of the strip as shown. Cut along the right edge of the ruler.

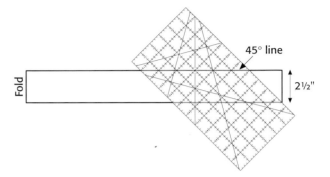

3. Refer to "Making the Templates and Marking the Background Pieces" on page 20 to trace template pattern G on page 78 onto frosted template plastic, and cut it out. Using double-stick tape, attach it to the wrong side of a 6"-wide rotary ruler as shown, making sure the angled edge is flush with the edge of the ruler.

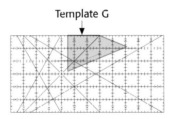

Template G

4. Place the ruler on the fabric strip so that the bottom edge of the template is aligned with the bottom edge of the fabric strip as shown. Cut along the right edge of the ruler.

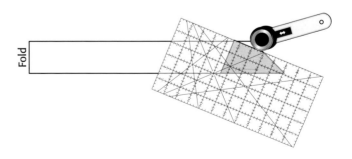

5. Reposition the template on the ruler as shown.

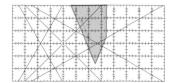

6. Place the ruler on the fabric strip so the edges of the template are aligned with the cut edges of the strip. Cut along the left edge of the ruler to produce 1 corner piece and 1 reversed corner piece.

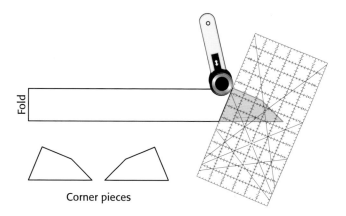

Corner pieces

Making the Templates and Marking the Background Pieces

Split Diamonds already have an accurate ¼" seam allowance and alignment dots marked on the foundation. The background pieces needed to complete the blocks must now be marked with compatible alignment dots to ensure accuracy, using the template patterns on pages 74–78.

1. Lay a piece of template plastic over the desired template pattern, and tape it down with masking tape to keep it from moving. Using a ruler and a fine-point permanent marker, trace the printed template onto the template plastic. Mark the solid lines, the grain line, all of the alignment dots, and the template letter on the template. The solid lines indicate the cutting lines; the dashed lines are the sewing lines and do not need to be marked on the template.

2. Cut out the template on the cutting lines, using a rotary cutter or sharp scissors. Punch out the alignment dots using a ⅟₁₆" hole punch. To prevent the templates from moving when tracing them onto the fabric, apply little sandpaper dots to the underside of the template, but take care not to cover the punched alignment dots.

3. Lay the correct template on the wrong side of the corresponding fabric piece, aligning all of the edges. Using a sharp pencil or fabric marker, mark the alignment dots. This also provides an opportunity to check the accuracy of your rotary cutting. If the piece does not fit the template exactly, trim the piece to size.

Making a Sample Block

You now know about all of the pieces you'll need to complete the blocks for the quilts in this book. But, before you dive into making a project, let's make a sample block to test out that newfound knowledge. The instructions here will make a Half-and-Half Star block.

Preparing the Units

1. Split the 2 Diamond Log Cabin foundation units you made previously (see "Piecing the Diamond Log Cabin Units" on page 13) into Twinkling and Twirling diamonds. Pair each Twinkling diamond with a Twirling diamond. Make 4 pairs.

Separate Twinkling Diamonds (left) and Twirling Diamonds (right) into 4 pairs.

2. From the background fabric, cut 1 square, 4¼" x 4¼". Cut the square in half twice diagonally to yield 4 quarter-square triangles (template A). Also cut 4 squares, 2⅝" x 2⅝" (template B). Refer to "Making the Templates and Marking the Background Pieces" on page 20 to make templates A (page 76) and B (page 74), and mark the alignment dots on the corresponding background pieces.

Assembling the Block

1. With right sides together and the Twinkling diamonds on top, place each pair of diamonds together as shown. Pin the diamonds together along the upper right edge at the alignment dots and at any matching seams (see "Tips for Success" on page 24). Sew along the stitching line, beginning in the seam allowance at the point of the diamond and ending at the lower right alignment dot. Do not sew into the seam allowance past the dot. Backstitch to secure the threads. If you are not sure if one more stitch will go beyond the marked dot, stop a little short of the dot. This will not cause a problem, but stitching too far will.

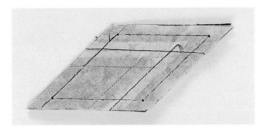

2. Set in a background quarter-square triangle between each pair of diamonds. To do this, place the triangle on top of the diamond unit, right sides together, as shown. Turn the pieces over so the diamond unit is facing up. Match the alignment dots along the upper diagonal edge and pin the pieces together. With the diamond on top, begin sewing on the sewing line, slightly ahead of the center alignment dot; reverse to the alignment dot and then stitch forward along the sewing line all the way to the outside edge of the diamond point.

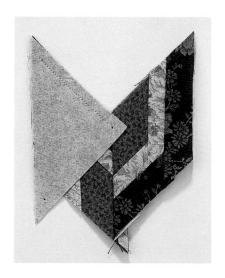

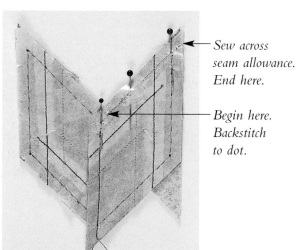

Sew across seam allowance. End here.

Begin here. Backstitch to dot.

3. Pin the remaining short side of the triangle to the opposite diamond's upper edge as shown, matching alignment dots. With the diamond on top, stitch along the sewing line, beginning at the outside edge of the diamond point and ending at the center alignment dot; backstitch.

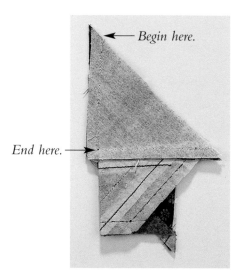

Begin here.

End here.

4. If you are using a foundation that can be torn away, remove the foundation of the Twinkling diamond in the seam allowance between the diamonds. Press the seam allowance toward the Twinkling diamond. Press the remaining 2 seams toward the background triangle. Pressing the seams toward the background pieces may seem unusual, but this will enable the piece to lie flat, and the points of the diamonds will remain nice and sharp.

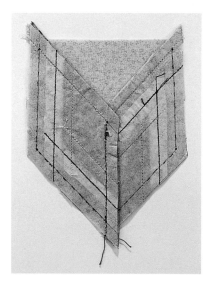

5. Pin 2 pairs of diamonds together, matching the alignment dots. Begin stitching at the outside edge of the seam allowance at the point of the diamonds and backstitch at the alignment dot as shown. Make 2.

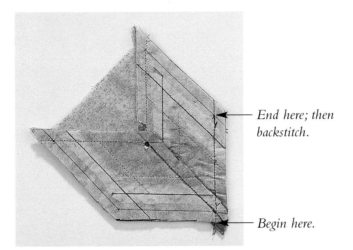

End here; then backstitch.

Begin here.

6. Refer to steps 2 and 3 to set the background squares into the opening between each stitched pair. Remove the foundation from the seam allowance between the 2 pairs, if possible, and press the seam toward the Twirling diamond. Press the set-in seam allowances toward the background squares.

Background square with one side stitched. Photo is shown from diamond right side; stitch from foundation side.

Half Star

7. Join the 2 halves of the star, matching and pinning the alignment dots and any matching seams. Because the seam allowances between diamonds were pressed in the same direction, the seams for the 2 halves will oppose perfectly, and the joints will be easy to match because of the ridges formed by the seams. Begin and end stitching at the alignment dots, backstitching at each dot.

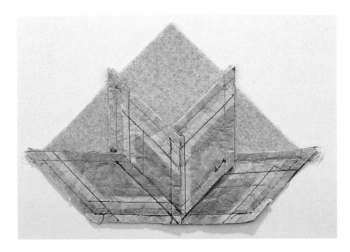

8. Set in the remaining 2 background squares in the same manner. Before pressing, remove the paper from the seam allowance. You can press this seam in one direction or open.

Remaining background squares with one side stitched.
Photo is shown from block right side; stitch from foundation side.

Finished Block

9. If you are using a foundation that can be torn away, carefully remove it.
10. Carefully press the finished block.

Tips for Success

- Apply spray starch to the background fabric before cutting it to keep the fabric firm and reduce stretching on the bias edges.

- When pinning two pieces together, it is important to match the alignment dots very carefully. Push the pin through the first dot, then through the dot on the underneath piece. Hold the two pieces tightly together while inserting the pin at a right angle to the seam line. This should eliminate any shifting that may occur during sewing. Remove the pins as you sew the pieces together, just before the machine needle reaches them.

- When sewing Split Diamonds together, it is vital to carefully match any seams within the diamonds that come together at the sewing lines.

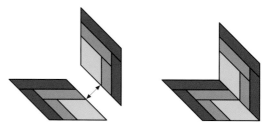

One Twinkling Diamond and One Twirling Diamond

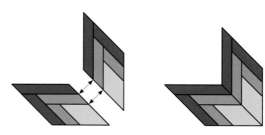

Two Twinkling Diamonds

- Press the seams of diamonds that have been sewn together toward the side of a diamond where no seams occur (a log, for example). This is not always possible, but when considering which way to press the seams, try to favor pressing them toward a log.

- When sewing Split Diamonds to background pieces or borders, sew with the diamonds on top, whenever possible, so you can use the marked sewing line on the foundation as a guide.

DESIGNING WITH SPLIT DIAMONDS

Split Diamonds are actually designs within a design; where normally whole diamonds are used in a traditional pattern, they are replaced with Split Diamonds. Because Split Diamonds are pieced Log Cabin diamonds, the opportunity for original design is increased many times.

All sorts of traditional blocks suggest themselves as candidates for Split Diamonds, the most obvious being the ever-popular Eight-Pointed Star and its many variations. Original designs can be made from any eight-pointed star pattern, from the simple Le Moyne Star, which has only one diamond in each star point, to the magnificent Lone Star, in which the eight diamond-shaped star points are made up of many small diamonds. Broken Star, Rolling Star, Blazing Star, and many more star variations all offer the potential and inspiration to produce interesting and unique designs.

Some traditional block patterns—such as Farmer's Daughter, Goose Tracks, and Churn Dash—aren't normally associated with the 45° diamond, but they also can be modified to suit Split Diamonds. With these types of blocks, you will probably have to alter the size of the original background pieces to suit 45° diamonds.

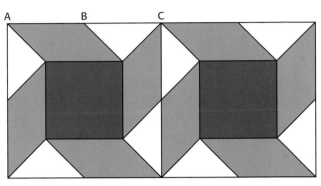

Traditional Churn Dash Block
The distance between A and B is the same as the distance between B and C. When joining two blocks, the seams match.

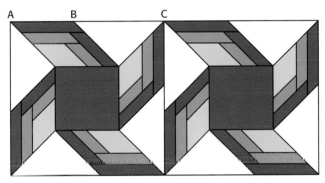

When using a 45° Split Diamond, the distance between A and B is smaller than the distance between B and C. When joining two blocks, the seams are offset.

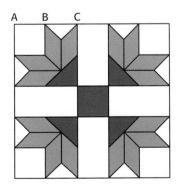

Traditional Goose Tracks Block
The distance between A and B is the same as the distance between B and C.

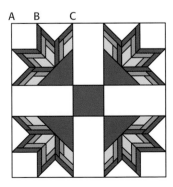

A design similar to the Goose Tracks block uses Split Diamonds. Here, the distance between A and B is smaller than the distance between B and C.

25

Arranging the Diamonds

You can make a design entirely of Twinkling diamonds, entirely of Twirling diamonds, or any combination of the two. Arrange Twinkling diamonds with all their small diamonds toward the center of a star, with their small diamonds toward the points of a star, or in an alternating design. Arrange Twirling diamonds clockwise or counterclockwise, or arrange them alternately, facing toward each other in pairs to form a Tulip pattern. Set this Tulip pattern either square or diagonally. Following are some of the many possible arrangements.

Stars with Single-Unit Points

Twinkling Star Block

Arrange 8 Twinkling diamonds with the small diamonds at the center of the star.

Reversed Twinkling Star Block

Arrange 8 Twinkling diamonds with the small diamonds at the outer points of the star.

Alternate Twinkling Star Block

Arrange 8 Twinkling diamonds so that the small diamonds alternate between the star points and the center.

Twirling Star Block

Arrange 8 Twirling diamonds with the small diamonds going counterclockwise.

Straight-Set Tulip Star Block

Alternately arrange 8 Twirling diamonds so that pairs of small diamonds meet at the background triangles.

Reversed Twirling Star Block

Arrange 8 Twirling diamonds with the small diamonds going clockwise.

Diagonally Set Tulip Star Block

Alternately arrange 8 Twirling diamonds so that pairs of small diamonds meet at the background squares.

Half-and-Half Star Block

Alternately arrange 4 Twinkling diamonds with the small diamonds facing the star center and 4 Twirling diamonds with the small diamond going counterclockwise.

Reversed Half-and-Half Star Block

Alternately arrange 4 Twinkling diamonds with the small diamonds toward the star point and 4 Twirling diamonds with the small diamonds going clockwise.

Stars with Multiple-Unit Points

That's already a lot of combinations, but it's just the beginning. Each diamond-shaped star point can be made from one diamond, as you saw in the previous examples that were based on the Le Moyne Star, or with four diamonds, nine diamonds, sixteen diamonds, and so on, depending on the design and size you need. The more diamonds that make up a star point, the more intricate the design becomes. Be aware that when star points are sewn together, a secondary design will occur at the seams. Again, you can make blocks with all Twinkling diamonds, all Twirling diamonds, or a combination of both. In the following blocks, which are based on the Virginia Star block, four diamonds are used to make each star point.

Twinkling Star Block

Arrange 32 Twinkling diamonds, 4 in each point, so that the small diamonds point toward the center of the star.

Twirling Star Block

Arrange 32 Twirling diamonds, 4 in each point, so that the small diamonds rotate counterclockwise.

Reversed Twirling Star Block

Arrange 32 Twirling diamonds so that the small diamonds rotate clockwise.

Star and Tulip Block

Use 16 Twinkling diamonds in one color combination and 16 Twirling diamonds in another color combination. Arrange the Twinkling diamonds so that the small diamonds point toward the center of the star. Arrange the Twirling diamonds so that pairs of small diamonds oppose each other.

Tip

You can also make Twinkling diamonds from one color combination and Twirling diamonds from another, but this is rather wasteful unless you are making two blocks in which you can alternate the colors.

Star and Diamond Block

Use 16 Twinkling diamonds in one color combination and 16 Twirling diamonds in another color combination. Arrange the Twinkling diamonds so that the small diamonds point toward the center of the star. Arrange the Twirling diamonds so that the small diamonds face each other.

Other Star Design Possibilities

Quarter stars (two star points), half stars (four star points), and three-quarter stars (six star points) can be combined or used alone to create more innovative designs. For examples, refer to "Star Flower" and "Before the Storm" on page 73.

Combining traditional whole diamonds with Split Diamonds also works well and adds another dimension to design possibilities. Use whole diamonds to make a chain along the points of a star (see "Wreathed Star" on page 69), to accentuate a ring of diamonds within a star, to emphasize the points of a star, or to alter the shape of a star (see "Sapphire Star" on page 43).

Traditional whole diamonds form a ring within a star.

Traditional whole diamonds emphasize the star points and center.

Altering the placement of the three fabrics when foundation-piecing the Log Cabin diamonds can also provide some interesting design elements. With just three fabrics, you can make six different Log Cabin diamonds, which in turn will yield different Twinkling and Twirling diamonds.

Designing Borders

Split Diamonds can also be used effectively in the border(s) of your quilt.

◆ Try using quarter stars or three-quarter stars at the corners of a plain border (refer to "Tulip Time" below and on page 35 and "Sapphire Star" below and on page 43).

Tulip Time

Sapphire Star

◆ Set single diamonds vertically (refer to "Garden Maze" below and on page 71) or horizontally (refer to "Amethyst Star" below and on page 69) and use plain half diamonds for the background pieces.

Garden Maze

Amethyst Star

◆ Make a "ribbon" border by setting quarter stars vertically and fill in with background squares and triangles (refer to "Wreathed Star" above right and on page 69), or set quarter stars horizontally to form a chevron or chain (refer to "Stained Glass" above right and on page 55 and "Starlight" on page 68). With chevron and

chain borders, half stars will automatically form at the corners when the borders are joined.

Wreathed Star

Stained Glass

◆ Create an extravagant border on a large quilt by using either half stars or whole stars (refer to "Lone Star Medallion" below and on page 60).

Lone Star Medallion

There will usually be a difference between the length of the pieced border strip and the edge of the quilt top it will be stitched to, because the pieces used in the border are different from the pieces used in the quilt. To compensate for the difference, simply insert a plain border between the quilt top and the pieced border. The easiest way to do this is to make the pieced border slightly longer than the quilt, then measure the length of the border and the quilt top edge it will be stitched to (side, top, or bottom). Divide the difference by two and add ½" for seam allowances. This measurement will be the width of the inner border, including seam allowances. If you find that the difference between the two measurements is too wide for one border, make two borders by dividing the measurement, either into two equal parts or by making one slightly wider than the other. Don't forget to add seam allowances to both borders.

Estimating Yardage

With foundation piecing, it's sometimes hard to know how much fabric you'll need. If you decide to add blocks to the quilts in this book or design your own quilts, these handy charts will help you estimate the yardage for the three fabrics needed to foundation-piece the Diamond Log Cabin units, and they'll tell you the number of strips you'll need to cut for the number of units needed. Cut all strips across the fabric width from selvage to selvage.

Center Diamond		
No. of Foundation Units	No. of 2½"-Wide Strips to Cut	Estimated Yardage
2	1	⅛ yd.
4	1	⅛ yd.
8	1	⅛ yd.
10	1	⅛ yd.
12	2	¼ yd.
16	2	¼ yd.
20	2	¼ yd.
24	3	⅜ yd.
28	3	⅜ yd.
32	3	⅜ yd.
36	4	⅜ yd.
40	4	⅜ yd.
44	5	½ yd.
48	5	½ yd.

Round 1		
No. of Foundation Units	No. of ⅞"-Wide Strips to Cut	Estimated Yardage
2	1	⅛ yd.
4	2	⅛ yd.
8	4	¼ yd.
10	5	¼ yd.
12	6	¼ yd.
16	8	⅜ yd.
20	10	⅜ yd.
24	12	⅜ yd.
28	14	½ yd.
32	16	½ yd.
36	18	⅝ yd.
40	20	⅝ yd.
44	22	¾ yd.
48	24	¾ yd.

Round 2		
No. of Foundation Units	No. of 1"-Wide Strips to Cut	Estimated Yardage
2	2	⅛ yd.
4	3	¼ yd.
8	6	¼ yd.
10	7	¼ yd.
12	9	⅜ yd.
16	12	⅜ yd.
20	14	½ yd.
24	17	⅝ yd.
28	20	⅝ yd.
32	23	¾ yd.
36	26	¾ yd.
40	28	⅞ yd.
44	31	⅞ yd.
48	34	1 yd.

FINISHING YOUR QUILT

Although each project gives specific instructions for finishing the quilt, you'll find some helpful information in this section.

Quilting

Split Diamonds can be quilted by hand or machine. Quilt all of the Split Diamonds "in the ditch," which means close to the seams along each log and around the outside edge of the small diamonds. Only quilt along one side of the seams, preferably on the side without seam allowances. It is not necessary to quilt along every seam, and you may find it difficult to quilt through seam allowances because of the thickness of several layers. Where seams meet at the center of a star, only quilt along alternate logs or three sides of the small diamonds; avoid the seam allowances. Leaving some logs unquilted in parts of a design will help them to stand out.

Large background pieces provide an opportunity to show off your quilting skills, either with a simple background design, such as cross-hatching, or a more elaborate design, such as a feathered heart.

Binding

With the exception of "Lone Star Medallion" on page 60, all of the projects in this book are bound using a double-fold binding in which the binding strip is folded in half lengthwise, wrong sides together, and stitched to the quilt edge. The binding is then folded to the quilt back and stitched in place.

For "Lone Star Medallion," a multifabric, single-fold binding is used. Once you've stitched together the fabric pieces to make the binding strip, align the binding and quilt raw edges, right sides together, and stitch the binding to the quilt. Press the unstitched long raw edge under ¼", then fold the binding to the wrong side, and stitch it in place.

Tip

Once you have completed the quilt top and added the binding, quilt around the outside edge, close to the binding, to give the quilt a neater finish and to help the binding lie flat.

TULIP TIME

◆ **Skill level: Easiest**

 This diagonally set Tulip design is based on the traditional eight-pointed star pattern called Harvest Sun in which each star point is made up of nine diamonds. The foundation units that make up the star points are made in two different fabric combinations. Using the dark green fabric for round 2 of one of the combinations helps to define the design. One block is all you need to make a nice-size wall hanging.

Materials

Yardage is based on 42"-wide fabric.

◆ 1 yd. pink-and-green print for foundation A (round 2 logs) and outer border

◆ ¾ yd. dark green print for foundation B (round 2 logs), inner border, and binding

◆ ½ yd. light green print for background

◆ ⅜ yd. cream print for foundation A (center diamonds) and foundation B (round 1 logs)

◆ ⅜ yd. pink print for foundation A (round 1 logs) and foundation B (center diamonds)

◆ 1⅛ yds. fabric for backing

◆ 35" x 35" square of batting

◆ Template plastic

◆ Foundation material

Cutting

From the light green print, cut:

1 square, 10¼" x 10¼"; cut the square in half twice diagonally to yield 4 quarter-square triangles (template C)

4 squares, 6⅞" x 6⅞" (template D)

From the cream print, cut:

2 strips, 2½" x width of fabric. From these strips, cut 12 center diamonds (see "Cutting the Center 45° Diamond" on page 12).

4 strips, ⅞" x width of fabric. From these strips, cut:
  ❖ 8 strips, 4" long, for log #1
  ❖ 16 strips, 4½" long, for logs #2 and #3
  ❖ 8 strips, 5" long, for log #4

From the pink print, cut:

6 strips, ⅞" x width of fabric. From these strips, cut:
  ❖ 12 strips, 4" long, for log #1
  ❖ 24 strips, 4½" long, for logs #2 and #3
  ❖ 12 strips, 5" long, for log #4

1 strip, 2½" x width of fabric. From this strip, cut 8 center diamonds (see "Cutting the Center 45° Diamond" on page 12).

From the pink-and-green print, cut:

8 strips, 1" x width of fabric. From these strips, cut:
  ❖ 12 strips, 5" long, for log #5
  ❖ 24 strips, 6" long, for logs #6 and #7
  ❖ 12 strips, 7" long, for log #8

4 squares, 2⅜" x 2⅜"; cut each square in half once diagonally to yield 8 half-square triangles (template E)

4 squares, 2⅝" x 2⅝" (template B)

4 strips, 4⅛" x 24¼"

From the dark green print, cut:

6 strips, 1" x width of fabric. From these strips, cut:
  ❖ 8 strips, 5" long, for log #5
  ❖ 16 strips, 6" long, for logs #6 and #7
  ❖ 8 strips, 7" long, for log #8

2 strips, 1½" x 22¼"

2 strips, 1½" x 24¼"

4 strips, 2½" x width of fabric

From the backing fabric, cut:

1 square, 35" x 35"

Assembling the Center Block

1. Using the patterns on pages 74 and 76, make templates B, C, D, and E. Use the templates to mark the alignment dots on the corresponding light green background pieces. Set the pieces aside.

2. Transfer the Diamond Log Cabin foundation pattern on page 10 to the foundation material. Make 20 foundations. Foundation-piece the A and B units, using the appropriate color center diamonds and round 1 and round 2 logs as shown. Make 12 foundation A units and 8 foundation B units.

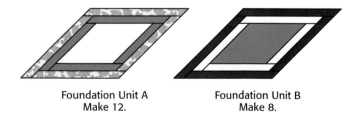

Foundation Unit A
Make 12.

Foundation Unit B
Make 8.

3. Split all of the units into Twinkling and Twirling diamonds. Set aside 8 foundation B Twinkling diamonds for the border corner blocks.

4. Arrange the remaining diamonds into star points #1 and #2 as shown. Pay particular attention to the placement and direction of each diamond, noting that the star points are mirror images of each other. To avoid confusion, assemble each star point separately. Join the diamonds into 3 rows of 3 diamonds each, matching the alignment dots and seams; sew on the sewing line. Press the seams in alternate directions from row to row. Stitch the rows together. Press the seams in one direction. Make 4 each of star point #1 and star point #2.

Star Point #1
Make 4.

Star Point #2
Make 4.

5. Stitch each star point #1 to a star point #2. Set in a light green background triangle between each pair of star points. Make 4.

Make 4.

6. Stitch 2 pairs of star points together; set in a light green background square between the 2 pairs to make a half star. Repeat with the remaining 2 pairs of star points.

7. With the center points matching, sew the 2 half stars together. Set in the 2 remaining light green background squares.

8. Press the block.

Adding the Borders

1. For the inner border, stitch a dark green 1½" x 22¼" strip to each side of the block. Press the seams toward the border. Sew the dark green 1½" x 24¼" strips to the top and bottom edges of the block. Press the seams toward the borders.

2. To make the outer border, sew the 8 Twinkling diamonds you set aside in step 3 of "Assembling the Center Block" into pairs as shown. Make 4.

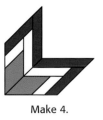

Make 4.

3. Set in a 2⅝" pink-and-green square between each pair of diamonds; stitch a pink-and-green half-square triangle to opposite sides of each diamond pair. Make 4 corner blocks. Carefully press each block.

Make 4.

4. Sew a pink-and-green 4⅛" x 24¼" strip to each side of the quilt. Press the seams toward the inner border. Sew a corner block to each end of the 2 remaining pink-and-green strips, making sure that the blocks are oriented so the star points will point toward the outside edges of the quilt when the borders are stitched in place. Press the seams away from the corner blocks. Stitch the borders to the top and bottom edges of the quilt top. Press the seams toward the inner border.

5. Carefully remove all of the foundation material if possible. Press the quilt top.

Finishing the Quilt

1. Layer the quilt top with batting and backing; baste.
2. Quilt the Split Diamonds in the ditch; leaving the dark green print logs unquilted in the center block will help them stand out. Quilt ¼" inside the background squares and triangles. Quilt a heart design in the background triangles and a rayed heart in the squares (see below). Quilt ¼" inside the outer edge of the inner border. Quilt ¼" inside the inner edge of the outer border, and quilt parallel lines ½" apart across the outer border to correspond with the seams on the Split Diamonds in the corner blocks.

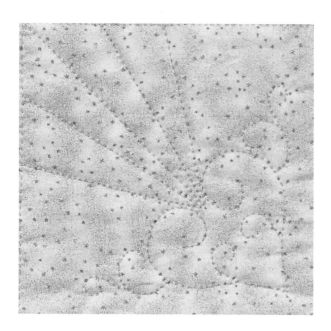

3. Trim the batting and backing even with the quilt top.
4. Bind the quilt edges with the 2½"-wide dark green strips.
5. Attach a hanging sleeve to the back of the quilt.

CHERRY BASKETS

◆ **Skill level: Easiest**

 By using Split Diamonds instead of diamonds cut from one fabric, a traditional Cactus Basket block has been transformed into an interesting and unique design: the Cherry Basket block. The Twinkling and Twirling diamonds could have been arranged in several different ways, but making all the blocks the same gives a more uniform look to the quilt. The blocks are set on point with corner triangles added in two shades of green. When alternate colors are joined, a secondary pattern forms.

Finished Quilt Size: 37⅝" x 37⅝"
Finished Block Size: 9⅜" x 9⅜"

Materials

Yardage is based on 42"-wide fabric.

- ¾ yd. navy blue print for foundation (round 1 logs) and outer border
- ⅝ yd. cream print for block background
- ½ yd. red print for foundation (center diamonds) and binding
- ½ yd. light green print for block corners
- ½ yd. dark green print for block corners
- ⅜ yd. multicolored print for baskets
- ¼ yd. medium green print for foundation (round 2 logs)
- ¼ yd. gold print for inner border
- 1⅜ yds. fabric for backing
- 42" x 42" square of batting
- Template plastic
- Foundation material

Cutting

From the cream print, cut:

5 squares, 4¼" x 4¼"; cut each square in half twice diagonally to yield 20 quarter-square triangles (template A). You will use 18 and have 2 left over.

9 squares, 2⅝" x 2⅝" (template B)

2 strips, 2" x width of fabric. From these strips, cut 18 segments, 2" x 4⅛" (template H).

5 squares, 3⅞" x 3⅞"; cut each square in half once diagonally to yield 10 half-square triangles (template I). You will use 9 and have 1 left over.

From the red print, cut:

5 strips, 2½" x width of fabric. From 1 strip cut 9 center diamonds (see "Cutting the Center 45° Diamond" on page 12); reserve the remaining strips for the binding.

From the navy blue print, cut:

5 strips, ⅞" x width of fabric. From these strips, cut:
- ❖ 9 strips, 4" long, for log #1
- ❖ 18 strips, 4½" long, for logs #2 and #3
- ❖ 9 strips, 5" long, for log #4

2 strips, 4½" x 30⅛"

2 strips, 4½" x 38⅛"

From the medium green print, cut:

6 strips, 1" x width of fabric. From these strips, cut:
- ❖ 9 strips, 5" long, for log #5
- ❖ 18 strips, 6" long, for logs #6 and #7
- ❖ 9 strips, 7" long, for log #8

From the multicolored print, cut:

5 squares, 3⅞" x 3⅞"; cut each square in half once diagonally to yield 10 half-square triangles (template I). You will use 9 and have 1 left over.

9 squares, 2⅜" x 2⅜"; cut each square in half once diagonally to yield 18 half-square triangles (template E).

From the light green print, cut:

8 squares, 5½" x 5½"; cut each square in half once diagonally to yield 16 half-square triangles (template J).

From the dark green print, cut:

10 squares, 5½" x 5½"; cut each square in half once diagonally to yield 20 half-square triangles (template J).

From the gold print, cut:

2 strips, 1¼" x 28⅝"

2 strips, 1¼" x 30⅛"

From the backing fabric, cut:

1 square, 42" x 42"

Assembling the Quilt Top

1. Using the patterns on pages 74, 75, 76 and 78, make templates A, B, E, H, I, and J. Use the templates to mark the alignment dots on the corresponding cream background pieces, multi-colored print pieces, and light green and dark green corner triangles. Set the pieces aside.

2. Transfer the Diamond Log Cabin foundation pattern on page 10 to the foundation material. Make 9 foundations. Foundation-piece the units, using the red diamonds for the center, the navy logs for round 1, and the medium green logs for round 2.

Make 9.

3. Split all of the units into Twinkling and Twirling diamonds.

4. Stitch each Twinkling diamond to a Twirling diamond as shown to make pair A and pair B. Make 9 of each pair.

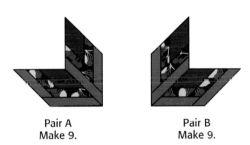

Pair A
Make 9.

Pair B
Make 9.

5. Set in a cream quarter-square triangle between each pair A and pair B.

6. Stitch a pair A to a pair B as shown to make a half star. Set in a 2⅝" cream square between each pair.

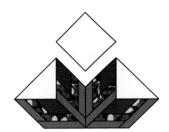

7. Sew a multicolored print 3⅞" triangle to the bottom of each half star. Press the seams toward the triangles. Make 9.

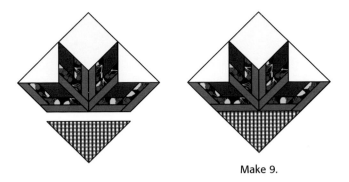

Make 9.

8. Sew the short edge of a multicolored print 2⅜" triangle to one end of each cream 2" x 4⅛" segment as shown. Press the seams toward the triangles. Make 18. Stitch the pieced strips to adjacent sides of the step 7 units. Press the seams toward the strips. Sew a cream half-square triangle to the bottom of each unit as shown. Press the seams toward the cream triangles.

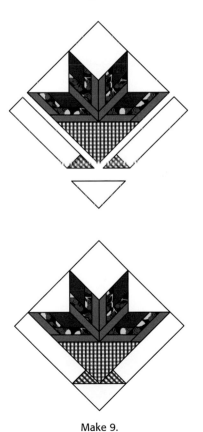

Make 9.

9. To complete the blocks, stitch a light green half-square triangle to each side of 4 units from step 8. Stitch a dark green half-square triangle to each side of the remaining 5 units. Press the seams toward the green triangles. Make a total of 9 Basket blocks, 4 with light green block corners and 5 with dark green block corners.

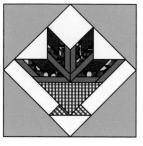 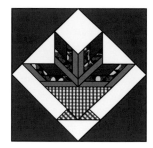

Make 4.   Make 5.

10. Alternately arrange the blocks into 3 horizontal rows of 3 blocks each as shown. Stitch the blocks in each row together. Press the seams in alternate directions from row to row. Sew the rows together. Press the seams in one direction.

Adding the Borders

1. For the inner border, sew the gold 1¼" x 28⅝" strips to the sides of the quilt top. Press the seams toward the border. Sew the gold 1¼" x 30⅛" strips to the top and bottom edges of the quilt top. Press the seams toward the border.

2. For the outer border, sew the navy 4½" x 30⅛" strips to the sides of the quilt top. Press the seams toward the border. Sew the navy 4½" x 38⅛" strips to the top and bottom edges of the quilt top. Press the seams toward the border.

3. Carefully remove all of the foundation material if possible. Press the quilt top.

Finishing the Quilt

1. Layer the quilt top with batting and backing; baste.

2. Quilt the Split Diamonds in the ditch. Quilt ¼" inside all of the background pieces, the basket, and the green corner triangles. I quilted an oval leaf shape in each corner triangle, as well. Quilt ¼" inside the outer edge of the inner border and ¼" inside the inner edge of the outer border. Quilt diagonal lines in each direction across the outer border.

3. Trim the batting and backing even with the quilt top.

4. Bind the quilt edges with the remaining 2½"-wide red strips.

5. Attach a hanging sleeve to the back of the quilt.

SAPPHIRE STAR

 Skill level: Moderate

 This quilt is based on the same star pattern that was used to make the "Tulip Time" wall hanging on page 35. By replacing some of the Split Diamonds with whole diamonds cut from the background fabric, the shape of the Harvest Sun design appears to change because the whole diamonds have blended into the background. The foundation blocks are made in two different color combinations, and the alternate star points are made in opposing colors. Three-quarter stars set at each corner round out this sparkling design.

Finished Quilt Size: 31" x 31"
Finished Center Block Size: 21¾" x 21¾"

Materials

Yardage is based on 42"-wide fabric.

◆ 1 yd. light blue print for background and outer border

◆ ¾ yd. dark blue print for foundation B (round 2 logs), inner border, and binding

◆ ⅜ yd. lilac print for foundation A (center diamonds) and foundation B (round 1 logs)

◆ ⅜ yd. blue print for foundation A (round 1 logs) and foundation B (center diamonds)

◆ ⅜ yd. purple print for foundation A (round 2 logs)

◆ 1⅛ yds. fabric for backing

◆ 36" x 36" square of batting

◆ Template plastic

◆ Foundation material

Cutting

From the light blue print, cut:

1 square, 10¼" x 10¼"; cut the square in half twice diagonally to yield 4 quarter-square triangles (template C)

4 squares, 6⅞" x 6⅞" (template D)

12 squares, 2⅝" x 2⅝" (template B)

4 squares, 2⅜" x 2⅜"; cut each square in half once diagonally to yield 8 half-square triangles (template E)

2 squares, 4¼" x 4¼"; cut each square in half twice diagonally to yield 8 quarter-square triangles (template A)

1 strip, 2" x width of fabric. From this strip, cut 8 diamonds and 8 reversed diamonds by folding the strip in half, right sides together, and then referring to "Diamonds" on page 18 (template K and K reversed).

4 strips, 4⅛" x 17½"

From the lilac print, cut:

1 strip, 2½" x width of fabric. From this strip, cut 10 center diamonds (see "Cutting the Center 45° Diamond" on page 12).

5 strips, ⅞" x width of fabric. From these strips, cut:
  ❖ 10 strips, 4" long, for log #1
  ❖ 20 strips, 4½" long, for logs #2 and #3
  ❖ 10 strips, 5" long, for log #4

From the blue print, cut:

5 strips, ⅞" x width of fabric. From these strips, cut:
  ❖ 10 strips, 4" long, for log #1
  ❖ 20 strips, 4½" long, for logs #2 and #3
  ❖ 10 strips, 5" long, for log #4

1 strip, 2½" x width of fabric. From this strip, cut 10 center diamonds (see "Cutting the Center 45° Diamond" on page 12).

From the purple print, cut:

7 strips, 1" x width of fabric. From these strips, cut:
  ❖ 10 strips, 5" long, for log #5
  ❖ 20 strips, 6" long, for logs #6 and #7
  ❖ 10 strips, 7" long, for log #8

From the dark blue print, cut:

7 strips, 1" x width of fabric. From these strips, cut:
  ❖ 10 strips, 5" long, for log #5
  ❖ 20 strips, 6" long, for logs #6 and #7
  ❖ 10 strips, 7" long, for log #8

2 strips, 1½" x 22¼"

2 strips, 1½" x 24¼"

4 strips, 2½" x width of fabric

From the backing fabric, cut:

1 square, 36" x 36"

Assembling the Center Block

1. Using the patterns on pages 74, 76, and 78, make templates A, B, C, D, E, K, and K reversed. Use the templates to mark the alignment dots on the corresponding light blue background pieces. Set the pieces aside.

2. Transfer the Diamond Log Cabin foundation pattern on page 10 to the foundation material. Make 20 foundations. Foundation-piece the A and B units, using the appropriate color center diamonds and round 1 and round 2 logs as shown. Make 10 *each* of foundations A and B.

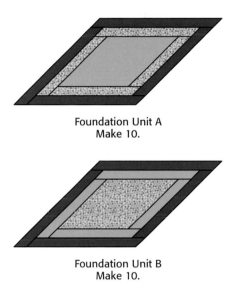

Foundation Unit A
Make 10.

Foundation Unit B
Make 10.

3. Split all of the units into Twinkling and Twirling diamonds. Set aside 8 Twinkling diamonds and 4 Twirling diamonds *each* from units A and B for the outer border.

4. Arrange the remaining foundation diamonds and light blue whole diamonds into star points #1 and #2 as shown. Join the diamonds into 3 rows of 3 diamonds each, matching the alignment dots and seams; sew on the sewing line. Press the seams in alternate directions from row to row. Stitch the rows together. Press the seams in one direction. Make 4 *each* of star point #1 and star point #2.

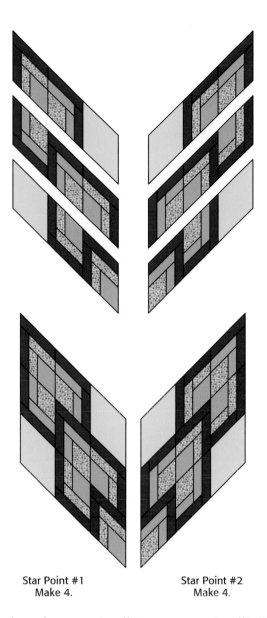

Star Point #1
Make 4.

Star Point #2
Make 4.

5. Stitch each star point #1 to a star point #2. Set in a light blue 10¼" quarter-square triangle between each pair of star points. Make 4.

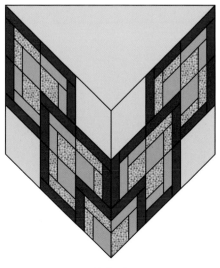

Make 4.

6. Pin 2 pairs of star points together; set in a light blue 6⅞" square between the 2 pairs to make a half star. Repeat with the remaining 2 pairs of star points.

7. With the center points matching, sew the 2 half stars together. Set in the 2 remaining light blue 6⅞" squares.

8. Press the block.

Adding the Borders

1. For the inner border, stitch the dark blue 1½" x 22¼" strips to the sides of the block. Press the seams toward the border. Sew the dark blue 1½" x 24¼" strips to the top and bottom edges of the block. Press the seams toward the borders.

2. To make the outer border, sew the Twinkling and Twirling diamonds you set aside in step 3 of "Assembling the Center Block" into pairs as shown. Make 4 *each* of pairs #1, #2, and #3.

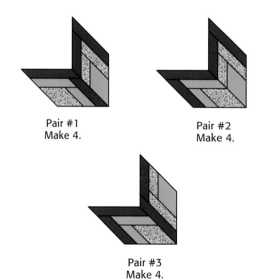

Pair #1
Make 4.

Pair #2
Make 4.

Pair #3
Make 4.

3. Set in a light blue 2⅝" square between each pair of diamonds. Stitch a light blue 2⅜" triangle to the Twirling diamond in pairs #1 and #3 as shown.

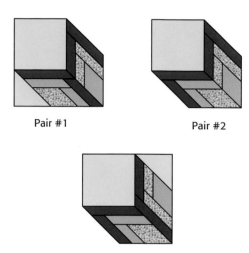

Pair #1

Pair #2

Pair #3

4. Sew a pair #1 and a pair #3 to the ends of a light blue 4⅛" x 17½" strip as shown. Press the seams toward the strip. Make 2.

Pair #3

Pair #1

5. Stitch the strips to the sides of the quilt top, orienting the strips as shown. Press the seams toward the inner border.

6. Stitch a pair #2 to each remaining pair #1 and pair #3 as shown. Set in a light blue 4¼" triangle between each pair to make a half star. Make 2 *each* of units 1-2 and 2-3.

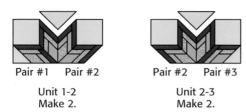

Pair #1 Pair #2   Pair #2 Pair #3

Unit 1-2   Unit 2-3
Make 2.   Make 2.

7. Sew a unit 1-2 and a unit 2-3 to the ends of one of the remaining light blue 4⅛" x 17½" strips as shown. Press the seams toward the strip. Make 2.

Unit 2-3   Unit 1-2

8. Stitch the strips to the top and bottom edges of the quilt top, orienting the strips as shown and matching the alignment dots and seams. Sew a light blue 4¼" triangle between the side and top and bottom border units, backstitching at the alignment dots. Press the seams toward the inner border.

9. Carefully remove all of the foundation material if possible. Press the quilt top.

Finishing the Quilt

1. Layer the quilt top with batting and backing; baste.
2. Quilt the Split Diamonds in the ditch, leaving the dark blue and purple logs around the center star unquilted to help them stand out. Quilt a random allover pattern in the background pieces. Quilt ¼" inside the inner edges of the inner and outer borders. Quilt a feather border in the outer border.

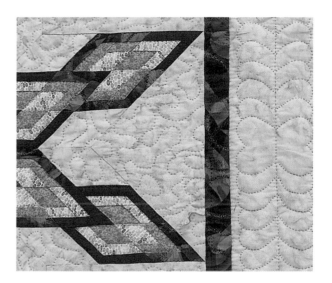

3. Trim the batting and backing even with the quilt top.
4. Bind the quilt edges with the 2½"-wide dark blue strips.
5. Attach a hanging sleeve to the back of the quilt.

CELESTIAL SAMPLER

 Skill level: Moderate

 Four different Virginia Star–based designs have been used to make this quilt: Twinkling Star, Reversed Twinkling Star, Spinning Star, and a variation on the diagonally set Double Tulip Star. Foundation-pieced Square-in-a-Square blocks in two different sizes have been used as cornerstones between the sashing strips and at the corners of the outer border. Using a larger print fabric in some of the diamonds, cornerstones, and outer border gives the quilt more visual texture and interest than it would have if the tone-on-tone and small print fabrics had been used on their own. The foundation blocks are made in three different color combinations.

Finished Quilt Size: 43½" x 43½"
Finished Block Size: 14½" x 14½"

Materials

Yardage is based on 42"-wide fabric.

- 1⅜ yds. dark pink print for foundation A (round 1 logs), foundation B (round 2 logs), sashing, and binding
- ⅞ yd. blue-and-pink print for foundation A (center diamonds), Square-in-a-Square blocks, and outer border
- ⅞ yd. navy blue solid for foundation B (round 2 logs), foundation C (round 1 logs), and Square-in-a-Square blocks
- ⅝ yd. light pink print for background
- ⅝ yd. yellow print for foundation A (round 2 logs), foundation C (center diamonds), and Square-in-a-Square blocks
- ⅜ yd. multicolored print for foundation A (center diamonds) and foundation B (round 1 logs)
- 3 yds. fabric for backing
- 48" x 48" square of batting
- Template plastic
- Foundation material

Cutting

From the light pink print, cut:

4 squares, 7¼" x 7¼"; cut each square in half twice diagonally to yield 16 quarter-square triangles (template L)

16 squares, 4¾" x 4¾" (template M)

From the multicolored print, cut:

1 strip, 2½" x width of fabric. From this strip, cut 8 center diamonds (see "Cutting the Center 45° Diamond" on page 12).

8 strips, ⅞" x width of fabric. From these strips, cut:
- 16 strips, 4" long, for log #1
- 32 strips, 4½" long, for logs #2 and #3
- 16 strips, 5" long, for log #4

From the dark pink print, cut:

4 strips, ⅞" x width of fabric. From these strips, cut:
- 8 strips, 4" long, for log #1
- 16 strips, 4½" long, for logs #2 and #3
- 8 strips, 5" long, for log #4

6 strips, 1" x width of fabric. From these strips, cut:
- 8 strips, 5" long, for log #5
- 16 strips, 6" long, for logs #6 and #7
- 8 strips, 7" long, for log #8

12 strips, 3" x 15"

5 strips, 2½" x width of fabric

From the blue-and-pink print, cut:

2 strips, 2½" x width of fabric. From these strips, cut 16 center diamonds (see "Cutting the Center 45° Diamond" on page 12).

9 squares, 2" x 2"

4 squares, 2½" x 2½"

4 strips, 4" x 37"

From the yellow print, cut:

6 strips, 1" x width of fabric. From these strips, cut:
- 8 strips, 5" long, for log #5
- 16 strips, 6" long, for logs #6 and #7
- 8 strips, 7" long, for log #8

1 strip, 2½" x width of fabric. From this strip, cut 8 center diamonds (see "Cutting the Center 45° Diamond" on page 12).

9 squares, 3¼" x 3¼"; cut each square in half twice diagonally to yield 36 quarter-square triangles

4 squares, 3¾" x 3¾"; cut each square in half twice diagonally to yield 16 quarter-square triangles

From the navy blue solid, cut:

12 strips, 1" x width of fabric. From these strips, cut:
- 16 strips, 5" long, for log #5
- 32 strips, 6" long, for logs #6 and #7
- 16 strips, 7" long, for log #8

4 strips, ⅞" x width of fabric. From these strips, cut:
- 8 strips, 4" long, for log #1
- 16 strips, 4½" long, for logs #2 and #3
- 8 strips, 5" long, for log #4

18 squares, 2⅞" x 2⅞"; cut each square in half once diagonally to yield 36 half-square triangles

8 squares, 3⅜" x 3⅜"; cut each square in half once diagonally to yield 16 half-square triangles

Assembling the Quilt Top

1. Using the patterns on pages 74 and 76, make templates L and M. Use the templates to mark the alignment dots on the corresponding light pink background pieces. Set the pieces aside.

2. Transfer the Diamond Log Cabin foundation pattern on page 10 to the foundation material. Make 32 foundations. Foundation-piece the A, B, and C units, using the appropriate color center diamonds and round 1 and round 2 logs as shown. Make 8 *each* of units A and C, and 16 of unit B.

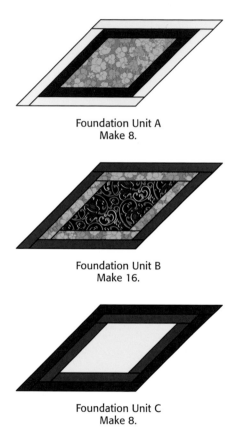

Foundation Unit A
Make 8.

Foundation Unit B
Make 16.

Foundation Unit C
Make 8.

3. Split all of the units into Twinkling and Twirling diamonds.

4. Arrange the diamonds into star points #1 and #2 as shown, following the combination given for each of the 4 blocks. Each block will use a different combination of diamonds to make the star points, but the assembly is the same. To assemble the star points, join each star point into 2 rows of 2 diamonds each, matching the alignment dots and seams; sew on the sewing line. Press the seams in alternate directions from row to row.

Stitch the rows together. Press the seams in one direction. Make 4 *each* of star point #1 and star point #2.

Star Point #1
Make 4.

Star Point #2
Make 4.

Twinkling Star Block Point Diagram

Star Point #1
Make 4.

Star Point #2
Make 4.

Reversed Twinkling Star Block Point Diagram

5. For each block, stitch each star point #1 to a star point #2. Set in a light pink quarter-square triangle between each pair of star points. Make 4 for each block.

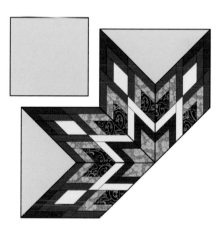

Make 4 for each block.

6. Sew 2 identical pairs of star points together; set in a 4¾" light pink square between the 2 pairs to make a half star. Repeat with the remaining 2 pairs of diamonds in each block combination.

Star Point #1
Make 4.

Star Point #2
Make 4.

Double Tulip Star Block Point Diagram

Make 2 for each block.

Star Point #1
Make 4.

Star Point #2
Make 4.

Spinning Star Block Point Diagram

7. With the center points matching, sew the 2 identical half stars for each block together. Set in the remaining light pink squares. Make 1 *each* of the Twinkling Star block, the Reversed Twinkling Star block, the Double Tulip Star block, and the Spinning Star block.

8. Press the blocks.

Twinkling Star
Make 1.

Reversed Twinkling Star
Make 1.

Double Tulip Star
Make 1.

Spinning Star
Make 1.

Adding the Sashing and Borders

1. Using the patterns on page 54, transfer the sashing Square-in-a-Square block foundation pattern and the border Square-in-a-Square block foundation pattern to foundation material. Make 9 sashing foundations and 4 border foundations. Foundation-piece the sashing foundations, using the navy-and-pink 2" squares for piece #1, the 3¼" yellow quarter-square triangles for pieces #2–#5, and the navy 2⅞" half-square triangles for pieces #6–#9. Make 9. Foundation-piece the border foundations, using the navy-and-pink 2½" squares for piece #1, the yellow 3¾" quarter-square triangles for pieces #2–#5, and the navy 3⅜" half-square triangles for pieces #6–#9. Make 4.

Make 9.   Make 4.

2. Arrange the Star blocks, 3" x 15" dark pink sashing strips, and sashing foundation blocks into horizontal rows as shown. Stitch the pieces in each row together; press the seams toward the sashing strips in each row. Stitch the rows together. Press the seams toward the sashing rows.

3. Stitch a navy-and-pink 4" x 37" strip to opposite sides of the quilt top. Press the seams toward the border. Sew a border foundation block to each end of the remaining 2 navy 4" x 37" strips. Stitch the strips to the top and bottom edges of the quilt top. Press the seams toward the border.

4. Carefully remove all of the foundation material if possible. Press the quilt top.

Finishing the Quilt

1. Cut the backing fabric in half widthwise. Sew the 2 pieces together along the long edges. From the pieced fabric, cut a square, 48" x 48", for the backing.

2. Layer the quilt top with batting and backing; baste.

3. Quilt the Split Diamonds and the Square-in-a-Square blocks in the ditch. Cross-hatch quilt the light pink background pieces. Quilt ¼" inside the long edges of the sashing strips; quilt a cable pattern along the sashing strips. Quilt ¼" inside the inner edge of the outer border, and quilt diagonal lines 1" apart across the border.

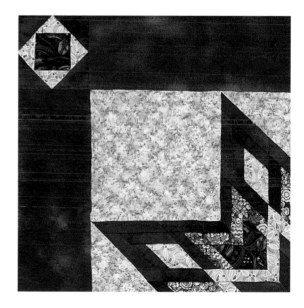

4. Trim the batting and backing even with the quilt top.

5. Bind the edges with the 2½"-wide dark pink strips.

6. Attach a hanging sleeve to the back of the quilt.

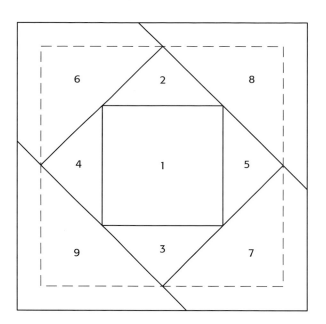

Sashing Square-in-a-Square
Foundation Pattern

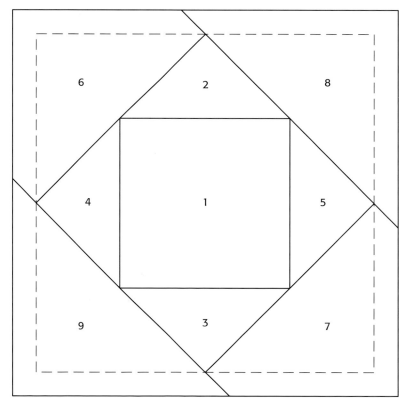

Border Square-in-a-Square
Foundation Pattern

STAINED GLASS

♦ ♦ ♦ **Skill level: Advanced**

 Red, blue, and gold silk douppioni are used to represent colored glass in this Starburst-based design. In some parts of the design, the foundation block has almost been re-created, but by using two or three different colors in the center diamond, a more intricate design emerges. A visual effect of light through the window is achieved by using the light gray in the diamonds and the background. The foundation blocks are made in three different color combinations, but only the color of the center diamond changes.

Finished Quilt Size: 35⅞" x 35⅞"
Finished Center Block Size: 27⅝" x 27⅝"

Materials

Yardage is based on 42"-wide fabric.

◆ 1⅝ yds. black print for outer border and round 2 of foundations A, B, and C

◆ 1½ yds. light gray print for center block background, outer border, and round 1 of foundations A, B, and C

◆ ⅝ yd. black solid for inner border and binding

◆ ⅜ yd. red solid for foundation A (center diamond)

◆ ⅜ yd. blue solid for foundation B (center diamond)

◆ ⅜ yd. gold solid for foundation C (center diamond)

◆ 1⅜ yds. fabric for backing

◆ 40" x 40" square of batting

◆ Template plastic

◆ Foundation material

Cutting

From the light gray print, cut:

2 squares, 9" x 9"; cut each square in half once diagonally to yield 4 half-square triangles (template N)

4 squares, 2⅝" x 2⅝" (template O)

36 strips, ⅞" x width of fabric. From these strips, cut:
  ❖ 72 strips, 4" long, for log #1
  ❖ 144 strips, 4½" long, for logs #2 and #3
  ❖ 72 strips, 5" long, for log #4

2 strips, 2⅞" x width of fabric. From these strips, cut 56 half diamonds (see "Half Diamonds" on page 18) (template F)

From the black print, cut:

48 strips, 1" x width of fabric. From these strips, cut:
  ❖ 72 strips, 5" long, for log #5
  ❖ 144 strips, 6" long, for logs #6 and #7
  ❖ 72 strips, 7" long, for log #8

2 squares, 3⅞" x 3⅞"; cut each square in half once diagonally to yield 4 half-square triangles (template I).

From the red solid, cut:

3 strips, 2½" x width of fabric. From these strips, cut 24 center diamonds (see "Cutting the Center 45° Diamond" on page 12).

From the blue solid, cut:

3 strips, 2½" x width of fabric. From these strips, cut 24 center diamonds.

From the gold solid, cut:

3 strips, 2½" x width of fabric. From these strips, cut 24 center diamonds (see "Cutting the Center 45° Diamond" on page 12).

From the black solid cut:

4 strips, 1⅝" x 30½"

4 strips, 2½" x width of fabric

From the backing fabric, cut:

1 square, 40" x 40"

Assembling the Center Block

1. Using the patterns on pages 77 and 78, make templates F, I, N, and O. Use the templates to mark the alignment dots on the corresponding light gray and black print background pieces. Set the pieces aside.

2. Transfer the Diamond Log Cabin foundation pattern on page 10 to the foundation material. Make 72 foundations. Foundation-piece the A, B, and C units, using the appropriate color center diamonds and round 1 and round 2 logs as shown. Make 24 of each foundation unit.

Foundation Unit A
Make 24.

Foundation Unit B
Make 24.

Foundation Unit C
Make 24.

3. Split all of the units into Twinkling and Twirling diamonds. Discard 8 Twinkling diamonds from unit B. Set aside 8 Twinkling diamonds and 32 Twirling diamonds from unit A, 32 Twinkling diamonds from unit B, and 8 Twinkling diamonds and 32 Twirling diamonds from unit C for the outer border.

4. Arrange the half diamonds and foundation diamonds into a wedge-shaped section as shown at right. Join the diamonds in each row first, matching the alignment dots and seams. Press the seams in alternate directions from row to row. Add the half diamonds. Press the seams toward the half diamonds. Stitch the rows together, adding the half diamond at the wedge upper right point last. Press the seams in one direction. Make 8.

5. Sew the wedge-shaped sections together in pairs. Make 4 pairs. Sew 2 pairs together to make a half sunburst. Make 2 half sunbursts. Matching the center seams, sew the 2 half sunbursts together.

6. Sew a light gray half-square triangle to alternate wedge-shaped sections as shown to form a square. Press the seams toward the corner triangles. Press the block.

Adding the Borders

1. Using the foundation diamonds you set aside in step 3 of "Assembling the Center Block," arrange the diamonds into border strips #1 and #2 as shown. To avoid confusion, assemble each border strip separately. Join the diamonds in each strip into 2 vertical rows of 7 diamonds each. Match alignment dots and seams; sew on the sewing line. Press the seams in each row in opposite directions. Sew the rows together. Press the seams in one direction. Make 4 each of border strips #1 and #2.

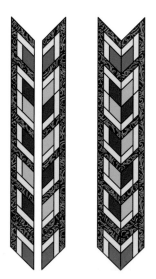

Make 1.

Border Strip #1
Make 4.

Border Strip #2
Make 4.

2. Set a light gray 2⅝" square into the inverted end of each border strip #1. Set the opposite edges of the square into the inverted end of a border strip #2. Make 4.

Border Strip #1 Border Strip #2

Make 4.

3. Measure 1⅝" from each end of each black 1⅝" x 30½" inner border strip, along one long edge, and make a mark. Make an angled cut on each end that goes from the marked point to the outermost point of the opposite edge as shown.

1⅝"

4. Stitch the angled strips to each foundation-pieced border strip as shown.

5. Sew the border units to opposite sides of the quilt, backstitching at the alignment dots at each corner. Press the seams toward the inner border. Stitch the remaining 2 border units to the top and bottom edges. To miter the corners, fold adjacent border strips so that they are right sides together. Sew from the alignment dot at the point of the diamonds to the alignment dot at the center block corner triangle. Backstitch at the beginning and end of the seam. Repeat for each corner. Sew a black print half-square triangle to each corner. Press the seams toward the triangles.

6. Carefully remove all of the foundation material if possible. Press the quilt top.

Finishing the Quilt

1. Layer the quilt top with batting and backing; baste.
2. Quilt the Split Diamonds in the ditch. Quilt a corner quilting pattern in each background triangle. Quilt in the ditch close to the inside edge of the inner border.

3. Trim the batting and backing even with the quilt top.
4. Bind the quilt edges with the 2½"-wide black solid strips.
5. Attach a hanging sleeve to the back of the quilt.

LONE STAR MEDALLION

 Skill level: Advanced

 In this Lone Star–based quilt, strong bands of color are achieved by placing two different fabrics of similar color and value next to each other. The Lone Star center block and Twinkling Star border blocks are made from Twinkling diamonds; the Tulip Star border blocks are made from Twirling diamonds. The pieced border uses three different colors to form a chevron pattern. The foundation blocks are made in five different color combinations.

Finished Quilt Size: 62¾" x 62¾"
Finished Center Block Size: 29" x 29"
Finished Middle Border Block Size: 7¼" x 7¼"

Materials

Yardage is based on 42"-wide fabric.

- 2⅞ yds. yellow solid for background and inner and outer borders
- 1⅜ yds. dark green print for foundation B (round 2 logs), foundation E (center diamonds), middle border background, and binding
- 1¼ yds. light green print for foundation D (round 1 logs), middle border background, and binding
- 1 yd. medium blue print for foundation A (round 1 logs), foundation D (center diamonds), middle border background, and binding
- ⅞ yd. dark blue print for foundations A and D (round 2 logs)
- ⅞ yd. navy blue print for foundations B and C (center diamonds), foundation E (round 1 logs), and binding
- ¾ yd. medium yellow print for foundation C (round 1 logs), foundation E (round 2 logs)
- ⅝ yd. light blue print for foundation B (round 1 logs) and foundation C (round 2 logs)
- ¼ yd. light yellow print for foundation A (center diamonds)
- 4¼ yds. fabric for backing
- 68" x 68" square of batting
- Template plastic
- Foundation material

Cutting

From the yellow solid, cut:
2 strips, 6½" x 51¼", along the lengthwise grain
2 strips, 6½" x 63¼", along the lengthwise grain
1 square, 13¼" x 13¼"; cut the square in half twice diagonally to yield 4 quarter-square triangles (template P)
4 squares, 9" x 9" (template Q)
2 strips, 4⅛" x 29½"

2 strips, 4⅛" x 36¾"
6 strips, 6½" x width of fabric

From the medium blue print, cut:
6 squares, 4¼" x 4¼"; cut each square in half twice diagonally to yield 24 quarter-square triangles (template A)
8 squares, 3" x 3"; cut each square in half once diagonally to yield 16 half-square triangles (template R)
8 strips, ⅞" x width of fabric. From these strips, cut:
  - ❖ 16 strips, 4" long, for log #1
  - ❖ 32 strips, 4½" long, for logs #2 and #3
  - ❖ 16 strips, 5" long, for log #4
2 strips, 2½" x width of fabric. From these strips, cut 16 center diamonds (see "Cutting the Center 45° Diamond" on page 12).

From the light green print, cut:
10 squares, 4¼" x 4¼"; cut each square in half twice diagonally to yield 40 quarter-square triangles (template A)
24 squares, 3" x 3"; cut each square in half once diagonally to yield 48 half-square triangles (template R)
32 squares, 2⅝" x 2⅝" (template B)
8 strips, ⅞" x width of fabric. From these strips, cut:
  - ❖ 16 strips, 4" long, for log #1
  - ❖ 32 strips, 4½" long, for logs #2 and #3
  - ❖ 16 strips, 5" long, for log #4

From the dark green print, cut:
8 squares, 4¼" x 4¼"; cut each square in half twice diagonally to yield 32 quarter-square triangles (template A)
16 squares, 3" x 3"; cut each square in half once diagonally to yield 32 half-square triangles (template R)
16 squares, 2⅝" x 2⅝" (template B)
12 strips, 1" x width of fabric. From these strips, cut:
  - ❖ 16 strips, 5" long, for log #5
  - ❖ 32 strips, 6" long, for logs #6 and #7
  - ❖ 16 strips, 7" long, for log #8
2 strips, 2½" x width of fabric. From these strips, cut 16 center diamonds (see "Cutting the Center 45° Diamond" on page 12).

From the light yellow print, cut:

2 strips, 2½" x width of fabric. From these strips, cut 16 center diamonds (see "Cutting the Center 45° Diamond" on page 12).

From the medium yellow print, cut:

8 strips, ⅞" x width of fabric. From these strips, cut:
- ❖ 16 strips, 4" long, for log #1
- ❖ 32 strips, 4½" long, for logs #2 and #3
- ❖ 16 strips, 5" long, for log #4

12 strips, 1" x width of fabric. From these strips, cut:
- ❖ 16 strips, 5" long, for log #5
- ❖ 32 strips, 6" long, for logs #6 and #7
- ❖ 16 strips, 7" long, for log #8

From the dark blue print, cut:

24 strips, 1" x width of fabric. From these strips, cut:
- ❖ 32 strips, 5" long, for log #5
- ❖ 64 strips, 6" long, for logs #6 and #7
- ❖ 32 strips, 7" long, for log #8

From the navy blue print, cut:

4 strips, 2½" x width of fabric. From these strips, cut 32 center diamonds (see "Cutting the Center 45° Diamond" on page 12).

8 strips, ⅞" x width of fabric. From these strips, cut:
- ❖ 16 strips, 4" long, for log #1
- ❖ 32 strips, 4½" long, for logs #2 and #3
- ❖ 16 strips, 5" long, for log #4

From the light blue print, cut:

8 strips, ⅞" x width of fabric. From these strips, cut:
- ❖ 16 strips, 4" long, for log #1
- ❖ 32 strips, 4½" long, for logs #2 and #3
- ❖ 16 strips, 5" long, for log #4

12 strips, 1" x width of fabric. From these strips, cut:
- ❖ 16 strips, 5" long, for log #5
- ❖ 32 strips, 6" long, for logs #6 and #7
- ❖ 16 strips, 7" long, for log #8

Assembling the Center Block

1. Using the patterns on pages 74, 75, 76, and 77, make templates A, B, P, Q, and R. Use the templates to mark the alignment dots on the corresponding yellow solid, dark green print, light green print, and medium blue print background pieces. Set the pieces aside.

2. Transfer the Diamond Log Cabin foundation pattern on page 10 to the foundation material. Make 80 foundations. Foundation-piece units A–E, using the appropriate color center diamonds and round 1 and round 2 logs as shown. Make 16 of *each* foundation unit.

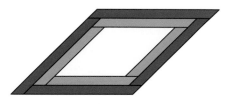

Foundation Unit A
Make 16.

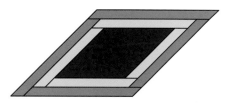

Foundation Unit B
Make 16.

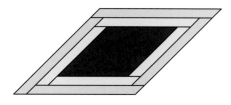

Foundation Unit C
Make 16.

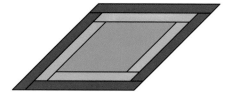

Foundation Unit D
Make 16.

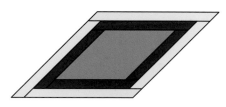

Foundation Unit E
Make 16.

3. Split all of the units into Twinkling and Twirling diamonds. Set aside all of the Twinkling and Twirling diamonds from unit E and all of the Twirling diamonds from units A, B, C, and D for the inner border.

4. Arrange the remaining diamonds into star points #1 and #2 as shown, paying particular attention to the log seam lines. Join the diamonds into 4 rows of 4 diamonds each, matching the alignment dots and seams; sew on the sewing line. Press the seams in alternate directions from row to row. Stitch the rows together, aligning the seam lines. Press the seams in one direction. Make 4 *each* of star point #1 and star point #2.

Star Point #1
Make 4.

Star Point #2
Make 4.

5. Stitch each star point #1 to a star point #2. Set in a yellow solid quarter-square triangle between each pair of star points. Make 4.

6. Stitch 2 pairs of star points together; set in a 9" yellow solid square between the 2 pairs to make a half star. Repeat with the remaining 2 pairs of star points.

7. With the center points matching, sew the 2 half stars together. Set in the 2 remaining yellow solid squares to complete the center block.

8. Press the block.

Adding the Borders

1. For the inner border, stitch the yellow solid 4⅛" x 29½" strips to the sides of the block. Press the seams toward the borders. Sew the 4⅛" x 36¾" strips to the top and bottom edges of the block. Press the seams toward the borders.

2. To make the middle border blocks, begin by sewing a light green half-square triangle to each dark green and medium blue half-square triangle. Make 32 light green–and–dark green squares and 16 light green–and–medium blue squares.

Make 32.

Make 16.

3. Use the foundation diamonds you set aside in step 3 of "Assembling the Center Block," the pieced squares from step 2, the 2⅝" squares, and the 4¼" quarter-square triangles to assemble the blocks, referring to the block diagrams below for the correct color combination. Refer to steps 5–8 of "Assembling the Center Block" to stitch the blocks together. Make 4 each of Tulip Star blocks #1–#5 and 4 Twinkling Star blocks.

Tulip Star Block #1
Make 4.

Tulip Star Block #2
Make 4.

Tulip Star Block #3
Make 4.

Tulip Star Block# 4
Make 4.

Tulip Star Block #5
Make 4.

Twinkling Star
Make 4.

4. Stitch the blocks together as shown to make the side borders and top and bottom borders. Make 2 of each border strip.

Tulip Star Block #4	Tulip Star Block #2	Twinkling Star	Tulip Star Block #1	Tulip Star Block #3

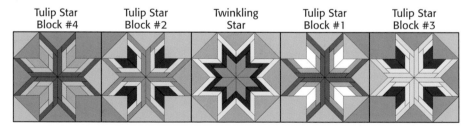

Side Borders
Make 2.

Tulip Star Block #5	Tulip Star Block #3	Tulip Star Block #1	Twinkling Star	Tulip Star Block #2	Tulip Star Block #4	Tulip Star Block #5

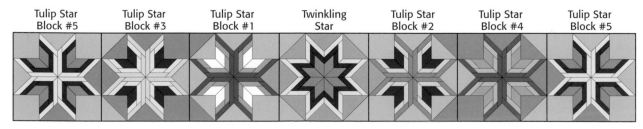

Top and Bottom Borders
Make 2.

5. Stitch the side borders to the quilt top as shown. Press the seams toward the inner border. Stitch the top and bottom borders to the quilt top as shown. Press the seams toward the inner border.

6. Sew the yellow solid 6½" x 51¼" strips to the sides of the quilt. Press the seams toward the outer borders. Sew the yellow solid 6½" x 63¼" strips to the top and bottom edges of the quilt top. Press the seams toward the outer borders.

7. Carefully remove all of the foundation paper if possible. Press the quilt top.

Finishing the Quilt

1. Cut the backing fabric in half widthwise. Sew the 2 pieces together along the long edges. From the pieced fabric, cut a square, 68" x 68", for the backing.
2. Layer the quilt top with batting and backing; baste.
3. Quilt the Split Diamonds in the ditch. In the center block, quilt a feathered heart in each background square and triangle, and crosshatch quilt the remainder of the background. Quilt ¼" inside both edges of the middle border, and quilt diagonal lines across the background pieces, following the direction of the chevron pattern. Quilt ¼" inside the inner edge of the outer border, and quilt a 4-line cable along the border.

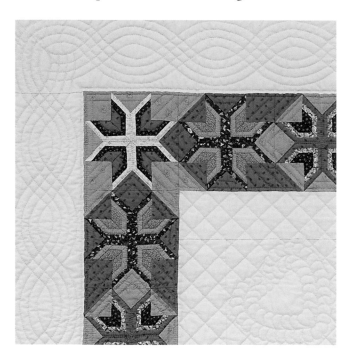

4. Trim the batting and backing even with the quilt top.
5. To make the pieced binding, cut 3½"-wide bias strips from the leftover medium blue, navy, light green, and dark green prints as shown. Sew the strips together along the long edges, and then crosscut the strip into 1½"-wide segments. Stitch the segments together, end to end, to make one continuous strip. Make as many pieced strips and cut as many segments as needed to make a binding strip that is at least 252" long when stitched together. Refer to "Binding" on page 34 to stitch the binding to the quilt edges, using the single-fold binding technique.

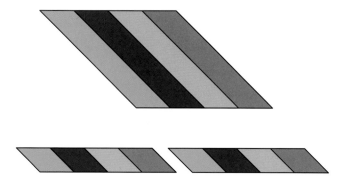

6. Attach a hanging sleeve to the back of the quilt.

Spring Garden by Pauline Johnston, 1999, Matlock, Derbyshire, England, 36½" x 43⅝".

Quarter stars combine with Attic Windows to make this original block. The blocks are set on point, with alternate rows containing either all Twinkling diamonds or all Twirling diamonds. Twinkling and Twirling diamonds set at opposing corners add more interest to plain borders. The foundation blocks are made in four different color combinations set diagonally across the quilt.

Starbright by Pauline Johnston, 1999, Matlock, Derbyshire, England, 38¾" x 38¾".

A few blocks left over from "Starlight" (below) were the inspiration for this coordinating wall hanging. The blocks are set on point with blue corners added to the Twinkling Stars and pink corners added to the Twirling Stars. The quilt is framed with a plain inner border, inset with triangles, and a Split Diamond chain border.

Starlight by Pauline Johnston, 1999, Matlock, Derbyshire, England, 72¾" x 87¼".

LeMoyne Star–based Twinkling and Twirling Stars are set alternately with plain squares in this pretty scrap quilt. Four foundation-pieced blocks will provide enough Split Diamonds to make one Twinkling Star block and one Twirling Star block. Each pair of stars is made from a different combination of pink and blue print fabrics. The design is divided diagonally, with Twinkling Stars set in one half of the quilt and Twirling Stars in the other half.

Amethyst Star by Pauline Johnston, 1999, Matlock, Derbyshire, England, 26½" x 26½".

A Harvest Sun–based design, this quilt demonstrates how a design can be significantly altered by color value. Note how the dark-value logs at the star points and surrounding the central star emphasize the design. The quilt is framed with a horizontal diamond border. The foundation blocks for this quilt are made in three different color combinations.

Wreathed Star
by Pauline Johnston, 2000, Matlock, Derbyshire, England, 52¼" x 52¼".

Whole diamonds make chains along the star points of this Rolling Star–based design. The star is made from all Twinkling diamonds, some forming stylized flowers and leaves, which appear to grow from the center star. The wreath is made from all Twirling diamonds, with half stars made from whole diamonds set at the corners. A ribbon border, made from pairs of Twinkling and Twirling diamonds, frames the quilt. The foundation blocks are made in two different color combinations.

Forbidden Orchard by Pauline Johnston, 2001, Matlock, Derbyshire, England, 20½" x 20½".

At first glance, the fruit-laden trees of this trio appear to be identical, but closer inspection reveals that, in fact, they are all different. The first tree contains only Twinkling diamonds; the second, both Twinkling and Twirling diamonds; and the third, only Twirling diamonds. All three designs are based on the traditional Forbidden Fruit Tree pattern. The foundation blocks are made in two different color combinations.

Shimmering Star by Pauline Johnston, 1999, Matlock, Derbyshire, England, 31" x 31".

Christmas prints and gold lamé make this Harvest Sun–based design an ideal decoration for the festive season. The light-tone fabric, used in the center Twinkling Star, blends in with the gold lamé at the star points, helping to define the stylized snowflake design. Quarter stars made from Twirling diamonds are set at the corners of the outer border.

Arctic Star by Pauline Johnston, 2000, Matlock, Derbyshire, England, 22½" x 22½".

It takes only eight foundation blocks in one color combination to make this small quilt. The design is based on the traditional North Star block.

Garden Maze by Pauline Johnston, 2002, Matlock, Derbyshire, England, 32" x 32".

Based on the Harvest Sun pattern, this quilt uses three different fabric combinations for the diamonds to add more interest. A visual effect of spaces is created by using one of the fabrics from the foundation blocks as the background. Vertically set Twinkling and Twirling diamonds, with half diamonds in the background pieces, make up the outer border.

Star and Tulips by Pauline Johnston, 2000, Matlock, Derbyshire, England, 28¾" x 28¾".

This star is colored with four light and four dark star points to create a shaded effect. To achieve this, the foundation blocks must be made in four different color combinations. Note how the darkest fabrics outline the Tulip design, making the tulips stand out and the center Twinkling Star recede.

Latticed Star by Pauline Johnston, 2001, Matlock, Derbyshire, England, 50" x 50".

This design is based on the traditional Lancaster Rose Star, where the center star is framed by a ring of diamond-shaped star points. The center star is made entirely of Twinkling diamonds, and the star points in the outer ring are made from either all Twinkling diamonds or all Twirling diamonds. The foundation blocks are made in two different color combinations, but because only one fabric is changed and the diamonds are all placed in the same direction within each star point, a lattice effect is achieved, with the new fabric forming a subtle band of stronger color across the widest part of the star points.

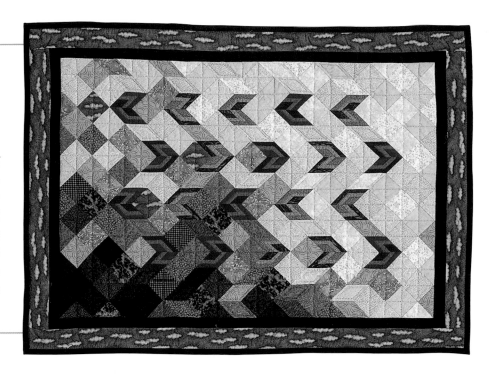

Before the Storm by Pauline Johnston, 2001, Matlock, Derbyshire, England, 40" x 29½".

In this original design, pairs of Twinkling and Twirling diamonds fly across a darkening sky of whole diamonds, squares, and triangles. A plain inner border and a cloud-print outer border frame the quilt. The foundation blocks are made in four different color combinations.

Star Flower by Pauline Johnston, 2001, Matlock, Derbyshire, England, 51½" x 51½".

Thirteen different color combinations are used to make the foundation blocks for this quilt. Some of the colors are chosen to blend; others are chosen to contrast. The design for this quilt was inspired by and based on an original Mariner's Compass design by Dutch quilter Ans Schipper. Where Ans used quarter-, half-, three-quarter, and whole Mariner's Compass blocks, I have used quarter-, half-, three-quarter, and whole stars.

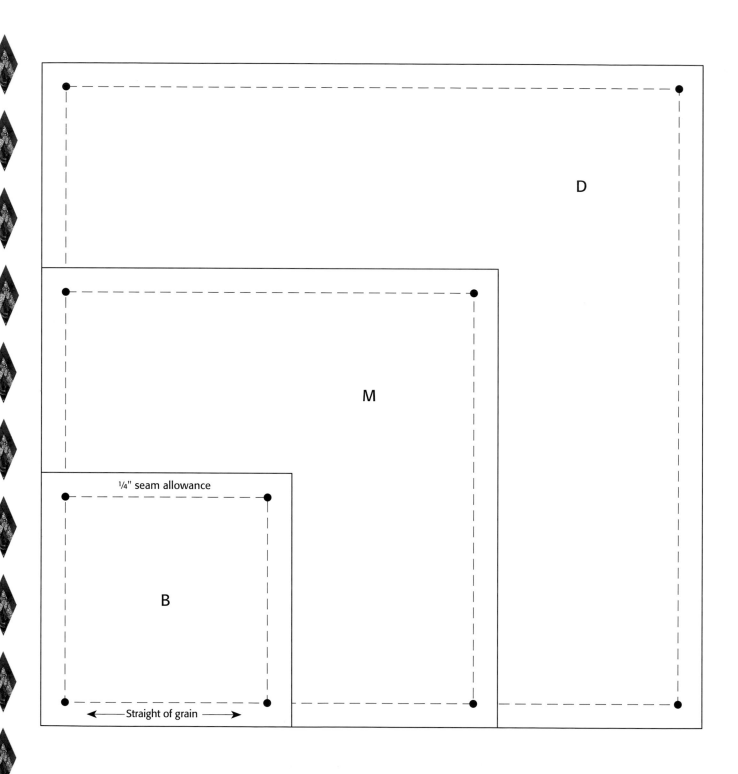

D

M

¼" seam allowance

B

← Straight of grain →

¼" seam allowance

Q

Flip pattern along broken line to complete template.

Straight of grain

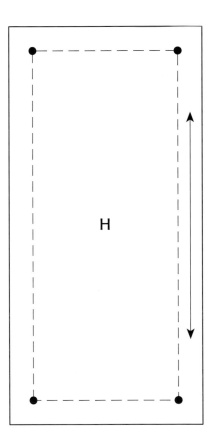

H

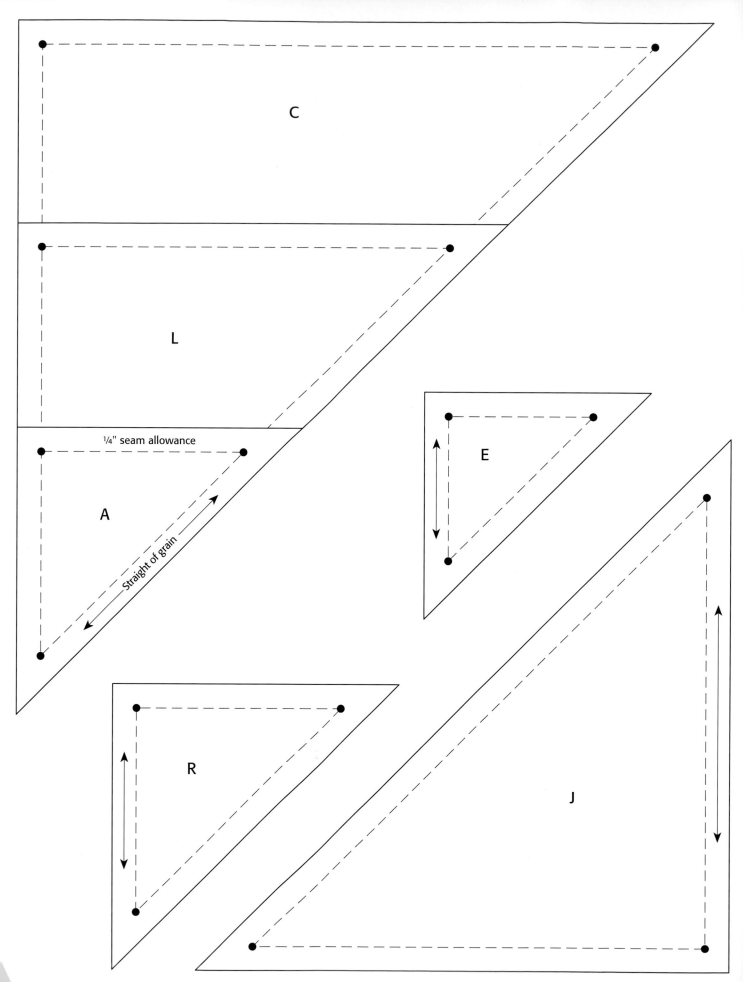

C

L

¼" seam allowance

A

Straight of grain

E

R

J

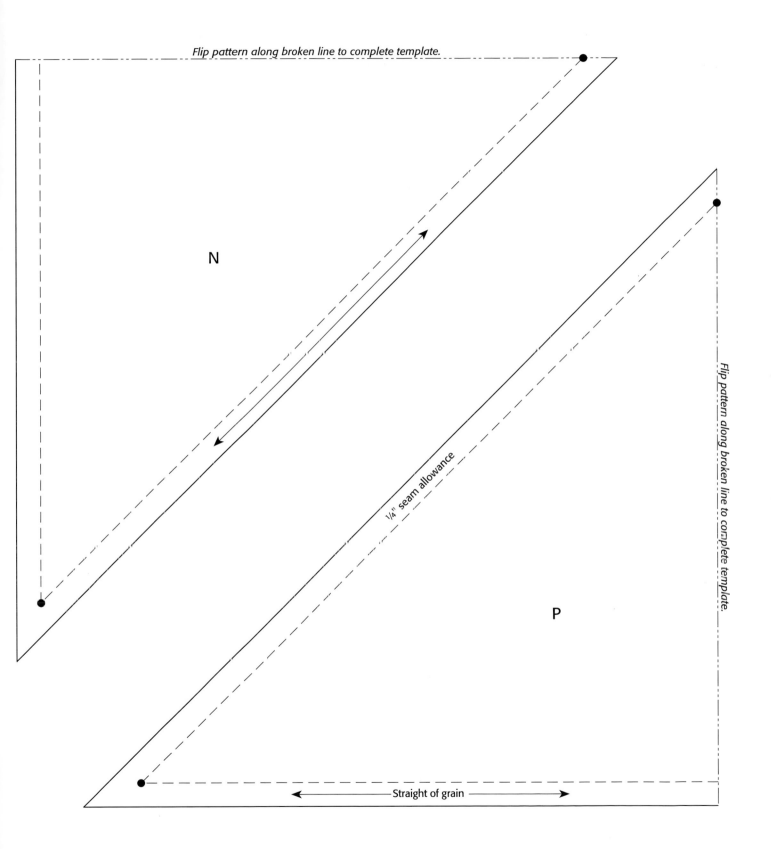

Flip pattern along broken line to complete template.

N

¼" seam allowance

P

Flip pattern along broken line to complete template.

Straight of grain

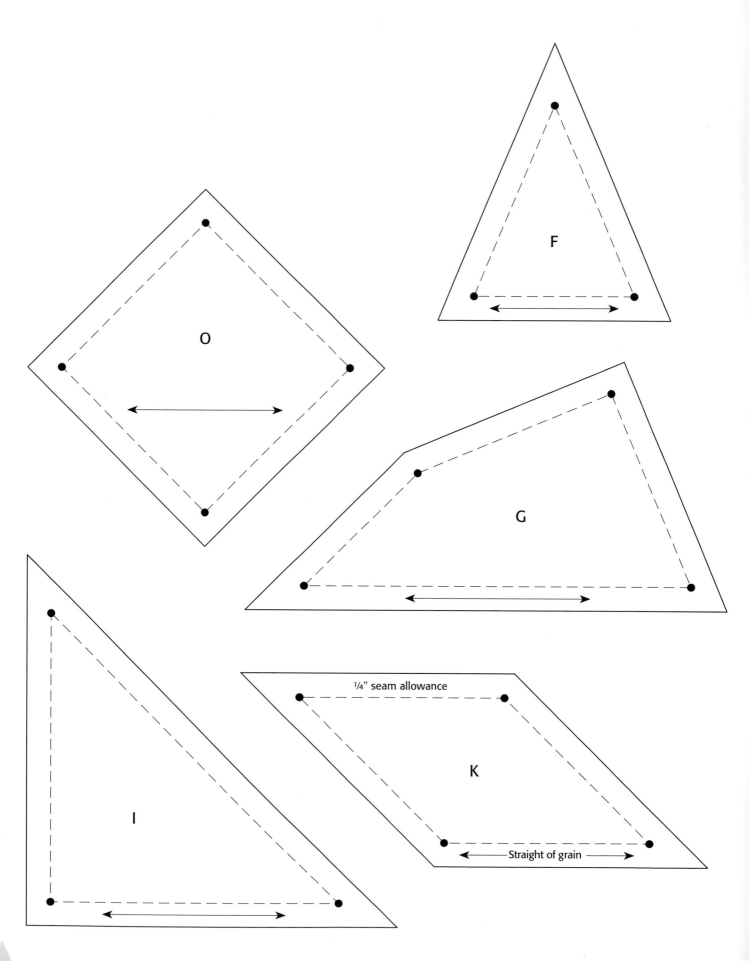

F

O

G

I

K

¼" seam allowance

Straight of grain

BIBLIOGRAPHY

◆ Beyer, Jinny. *Patchwork Patterns.* McLean, Va.: EPM Publications, Inc., 1979.

◆ Wien, Carol Anne. *The Log Cabin Quilt Book.* England: Westbridge Books for Readers Union Ltd., 1984.

◆ Martin, Judy. *Shining Star Quilts.* Golden, Co.: Leman Publications, Inc., 1987.

◆ Reis, Sherry. *Eight-Pointed Stars.* Bothell, Wash.: That Patchwork Place, 1999.

About the Author

Pauline Johnston's interest in sewing began at a very early age, when her mother, an expert seamstress, made beautiful sequined and beaded gowns for ballroom dancers and stage artists.

Although Pauline is proficient in all types of needlework, it wasn't until 1978, while watching the BBC television program *Discovering Patchwork,* that she was inspired to make her first quilt, a Lone Star lap quilt with huge diamonds. That was just the beginning of her fascination with quilting and, in particular, diamonds.

During the late 1980s, Pauline made quilts full-time and won many awards at major British quilt shows. In 1989, she opened her own patchwork shop, where she also gave lessons in quilting and made quilts on commission. What had begun as a hobby turned into a full-time business. Pauline's designs have regularly been featured in British publications, and her quilts have appeared on the cover of *Popular Patchwork,* a British quilting magazine.

Pauline has three grown sons and four grandchildren. She lives in Matlock, England, the gateway to the beautiful Peak District National Park. Now retired, Pauline has at last found the time to experiment with Log Cabin diamonds and to fulfill her lifelong ambition of writing a book.